BABYLON MYSTERY RELIGION

ANCIENT AND MODERN

BY RALPH WOODROW

COPYRIGHT 1966 ©

First Printing, Dec. 1966
Second Printing, Nov. 1968
Third Printing, Sept. 1969
Fourth Printing, June 1970
Fifth Printing, June 1971
Sixth Printing, May 1972
Seventh Printing, May 1973
Eighth Printing, April 1974

RALPH WOODROW EVANGELISTIC ASSOCIATION, INC.

P. O. BOX 124

RIVERSIDE, CALIFORNIA 92502

"Beloved, when I gave all diligence
to write unto you of the common salvation, it was needful for me to write
unto you, and exhort you that ye should
earnestly contend for the faith which
was once delivered unto the saints."

Printed in the United States of America

Contents

CHAPTER   PAGE

1. BABYLON—SOURCE OF FALSE RELIGION. Babylon's beginning—Nimrod, its first king—a mighty hunter—a rebel against God—his wife Semiramis —her child Tammuz—counterfits. A Biblical and historical account of how Babylonian paganism spread to the nations, was absorbed into the Roman Empire, and was finally mixed with Christianity at Rome—a mixture that produced the great falling away. 7

2. MOTHER AND CHILD WORSHIP. Queen Semiramis and her god-child Tammuz—how their worship developed under different names and forms in various countries—how it was mixed into the doctrines of the fallen church. Pagan titles applied to Mary. 13

3. MARY WORSHIP. Undue prominence given to Mary in the church of the falling away. The immaculate conception, the perpetual virginity, and Assumption of Mary theories considered in the light of the scriptures. The Rosary—its origin and history. 21

4. SAINTS, SAINTS' DAYS, AND SYMBOLS. Who are the saints? Are we to pray to them? Saint worship shown to be a continuation of the pagan devotion to the gods and goddesses of paganism. The use of idols, images, pictures as objects of worship. The aureole. 30

5. OBELISKS, TEMPLES, AND TOWERS. Significance of the ancient obelisks —their use in front of pagan temples—the obelisk in front of St. Peter's in Rome. The history of the Vatican Hill. Elaborate and expensive church buildings. The tower of Babel—religious towers. 39

6. IS THE CROSS A CHRISTIAN SYMBOL? The wide-spread use of the cross symbol—its ancient origin—its history among pagan tribes—its various forms and their significance. 49

7. CONSTANTINE AND THE CROSS. The cross vision at Milvian Bridge. Constantine's "conversion" shown to be a hoax. The story of Helena's discovery of the "true" cross considered. 57

8. THE RELICS OF ROMANISM. Pieces of the true cross and other relics examined—many shown to be fakes. The use of relics to "consecrate" a church—a pagan superstition. The origin of the idea. 62

9. RELIGIOUS FRAUD. Pilgrimages—Indulgence selling—Tetzel's sales in Germany—Luther—the Reformation. Purgatory—its origin and legends— paying for prayers. Molech worship. 66

10. WAS PETER THE FIRST POPE? Equality stressed by Christ. "On this rock I will build my church." Peter and the Popes compared. Peter's ministry compared to Paul's. Did Peter ever go to Rome? 75

11. PAGAN ORIGIN OF PAPAL OFFICE. The supreme pontiffs of paganism —the peter-roma, high priest of the Mysteries—the mystic "keys"—Janus —the tiara—the fish-god mitre—Dagon worship—the pallium—Peter's "chair"—statue of Jupiter renamed as Peter—kissing an idol—carrying an idol—papal processions—the fabelli "fans.". 80

12. PAPAL IMMORALITY. The unholy history of the papal office. Luther's visit to Rome. The female Pope. 94

13. ARE POPES INFALLIBLE? The Council of 1870. The trial of Formosus and Steven. Contradictions to the "infallibility" theory presented. Christ and the Popes compared. The mystic number 666. 101

14. THE INHUMAN INQUISITION. Persecution of protestants. The rack, the iron virgin, and other torture instruments described. Persecutions at Beziers, Lavaur, Orange, Paris, etc. 106

15. "LORDS OVER GOD'S HERITAGE." Cardinals—the origin of their office —their red garments. Bishops—the scriptural and traditional views compared. The "clergy"—church government—the ministry of elders in the local church. Religious titles. 111

16. AN UNMARRIED PRIESTHOOD. The celibacy doctrine of Babylon—its history—and immorality. The confessional—its origin and purpose. Priests in black garments. The sun-symbol tonsure. 119

17. THE MASS. Transubstantiation—its meaning, origin, and history. The "finished" work at Calvary contrasted to the mass. The monstrance, the round "host", a description of round sun-symbols and their use in paganism, the mystic letters I. H. S., the Mystery drama. The Lord's supper and the Mass compared. 126

18. THREE DAYS AND NIGHTS. The sign of Jonas. Was Christ crucified on a Friday? On what day was the resurrection? 141

19. FISH, FRIDAY, AND THE SPRING FESTIVAL. The fish, a fertility symbol—its association with the Mother Goddess and Friday. The Easter festival—eggs, rabbits, and cross buns. Sunrise services—"weeping for Tammuz"—Lent. 150

20. THE WINTER FESTIVAL. At what season was Christ born? The Saturnalia —gifts, trees, and customs. St. John's Day. Assumption Day. Candlemass Day. How pagan days were continued in the fallen church, renamed, and given the outer appearance of Christianity. 160

21. THE MYSTERY OF THE MIXTURE. A brief review of the mixture—how it was hidden—mixtures in the Old Testament compared. True Christianity must be based on the Bible, not tradition. Salvation only through Christ. 169

BIBLIOGRAPHY and acknowledgements. 176

5

THE POPE CELEBRATING MASS AT THE HIGH ALTAR OF ST. PETER'S CHURCH IN ROME. Do Popes and priests really have power to change bread and wine into the flesh and blood of Christ during the mysterious Mass ritual? See Chapter Seventeen.

CHAPTER ONE

Babylon-Source of False Religion

THE MYSTERY RELIGION of Babylon has been symbolically described in the last book of the Bible as an ill-famed woman. In vision, the Apostle John saw a woman "arrayed in purple and scarlet colour, and decked with gold and precious stones and pearls, having a golden cup in her hand full of abominations and filthiness of her fornication: and upon her forehead was a name written, MYSTERY, BABYLON THE GREAT, THE MOTHER OF HARLOTS AND ABOMINATIONS OF THE EARTH" (Revelation 17:1-6).

Now what is the meaning of this unusual vision that was given to John? It is well known that in the symbolic language of the Bible, a woman pictures a church. The true church, for example, is likened to a bride, a chaste virgin, a woman without spot or blemish (Eph. 5:27; Rev. 19:7, 8). But in striking contrast to the true church, the woman of our text is spoken of as an unclean woman, a defiled woman, or to use the Bible wording—which is sometimes very plain—she is a whore. It is evident then that the church system here described is a counterfeit system—a defiled and *fallen* church! In big capital letters, the Bible calls her: "MYSTERY BABYLON."

When John was inspired to write the Revelation, Babylon—as a city—had already been destroyed and left in ruins. It has remained a desolate waste ever since—inhabited only by wild animals—even as the prophets foretold.  (Isaiah 13:19-22; Jer. 51:62). But though the city of Babylon was destroyed, we shall see that the *religion* of Babylon continued on and was well represented in many nations of the world. And since John was speaking of a church, a *religion*, under the sym-

7

bol of a woman named Babylon, it is evident that the reference is to Babylonish religion. But just what was the religion of ancient Babylon? How did it all begin? And what significance does it hold in modern times?

Let us turn the pages of time back to the period shortly after the Flood. In those days, men began to migrate from the east, "and it came to pass, as they journeyed from the east, that they found a plain in the land of Shinar; and they dwelt there"(Gen. 11:2). It was in this land of Shinar that the City of Babylon was built and this land became known as Babylonia or later as Mesopotamia.

Here the Euphrates and Tigris rivers had built up rich deposits of earth that could produce crops in abundance. But there were certain disadvantages here which the people faced. The land was overrun with *wild animals* which were a constant threat to the safety and peace of the inhabitants. (Cp. Exodus 23:29, 30). Obviously anyone who could successfully provide protection from these wild beasts would receive great acclaim from the people.

And so at this point, a large powerfully built man by the name of Nimrod appeared on the scene. He became famous as a mighty HUNTER against the wild animals. The Bible tells us: "And Cush begat Nimrod: he began to be a MIGHTY ONE in the earth. He was a MIGHTY HUNTER before the LORD: wherefore it is said, Even as Nimrod the mighty hunter before the LORD"(Gen. 10:8, 9). Now there is a very significant meaning in these verses—a meaning that is seldom noticed:

It was Nimrod's success as a "mighty hunter" that caused him to become famous among those primitive people. As the scripture declares, he became "a mighty one" in the earth—a famous leader in worldly affairs. "Nimrod was so powerful, and the impression which his achievements made upon the minds of men so great, that the East is filled even to the present time with traditions of his extraordinary career."[1]

Gaining this prestige among the people, Nimrod devised a better means of protection. Instead of constantly fighting the wild beasts, why not organize the people into cities and surround them with walls of protection? Then why not organize these cities into a KINGDOM and appoint a king to rule over them? Evidently this was the thinking of Nimrod, for the Bible tells us that he organized such a kingdom! "And the beginning of his kingdom was Babel, and Erech, and Accad, and Calneh, in the land of Shinar"(Gen. 10:10). And so the kingdom of Nimrod became established and is the first kingdom mentioned in the Bible.

1. Ancient History in Bible Light, p. 54.

All of these advances made by Nimrod might have been well and good, but Nimrod was an *ungodly ruler*. The scripture says that he was "a mighty one." Not only does this indicate that he became famous and politically powerful, but the expression also has a hostile meaning. The expression comes from the Hebrew word "gibor" which means TYRANT; while the name Nimrod means "let us rebel." As THE JEWISH ENCYCLOPEDIA says, Nimrod was "he who made all the people rebellious against God."[1]

This same rebellious nature of Nimrod may also be seen from the expression that he was a mighty hunter "BEFORE the Lord." The word "before", in this instance, also carries a hostile meaning. In other words, Nimrod set himself up BEFORE God, the word "before" being the translation of a Hebrew word meaning "AGAINST" the LORD.[2]

But not only was Nimrod against the true God, he was also a priest of devil-worship and of heathenism of the worse kind, as we shall see. Then finally, Nimrod, the priest-king of Babylon, died. According to the old stories, his body was cut into pieces, burnt, and the pieces were sent to various areas. Similar practices are mentioned even in the Bible (Judges 19:29; 1 Samuel 11:7). The death of Nimrod was greatly mourned by the people of Babylon. But though Nimrod had died, the Babylonian religion of which he played a prominent part, continued on and developed further under the leadership of his wife.

After Nimrod's death, his wife, Queen Semiramis, claimed that he was now the Sun-god. And later, when this adulterous and idolatrous woman gave birth to an illegitimate son, she claimed that this son, Tammuz by name, was Nim-rod reborn. (The accompanying cut shows the way Tammuz came to be represented in Classical Art.) Now the queen-Mother of Tammuz had no doubt heard the prophecy of the coming Messiah to be born of a woman, for this truth was known from the earliest times (See Gen. 3:15). Satan had first seduced a woman, Eve; but later through a woman was to come the saviour —our Lord Jesus Christ. Satan, the great counterfeiter, also knew much about the Divine Plan. Thus, he began to set up counterfeits of the true plan centuries before Jesus came. Queen Semiramis, as

1. Vol. 9, p. 309.
2. See Strong's Concordance; cp. Num. 16:2; 1 Chron. 14:8; 2 Chron. 15:10

9

an instrument in Satan's hands, claimed that her son was super-naturally conceived and that he was the promised seed, the "sav-iour." However, not only was the child worshipped, but the wom-an, the **MOTHER**, was also worshipped as much (or more) than the son! As we will see in the pages that follow, Nimrod, Sem-iramis, and Tammuz were used as puppets in Satan's hand to produce false religion--though often appearing as the true!--and this corrupt system filled the world.

Much of the Babylonian worship was carried on through mys-terious *symbols*—thus it was a "Mystery" religion. The golden calf, for example, was a symbol of Tammuz, son of the Sun-god. Since Nimrod was believed to be the Sun-god or Baal, fire was considered as his earthly representation. Thus, as we shall see, candles and ritual fires were lighted in his honour. In other forms, Nimrod was symbolized by sun-symbols, fish, trees, pillars, and animals.

Centuries later, Paul gave a description which perfectly fits the course that the people of Babylon followed: "When they knew God, they glorified him not as God...but became vain in their imaginations, and their foolish heart was darkened. Professing themselves to be wise, they became fools, and changed the glory of the uncorruptible God into an IMAGE made like to corruptible man, and to birds, and fourfooted beasts, and creeping things... they changed the truth of God into a lie, and worshipped and ser-ved the CREATURE more than the CREATOR...for this cause God gave them up unto vile affections"(Rom. 1:21-26).

This system of idolatry spread from Babylon to the nations, for it was from this location that men were scattered over the face of the earth (Gen. 11:9). As they went from Babylon, they took their worship of the Babylonian family and its various mys-tery symbols with them. And so, to this day, we find evidence of the religion of Babylon—in one form or another--in all the false religions of earth! Truly Babylon was the "Mother"—the originator—of false religion and the idolatry that has spread throughout the earth. As the scriptures declare, all nations drank from her cup of false doctrine. (Jer. 51:7; Rev. 18:3).

In addition to the scriptural proof that Babylon was the Mother, the source, of pagan religion, we also have the testimony of noted historians. Herodotus, the world traveler and historian of an-tiquity, for example, witnessed the Mystery religion and its rites in numerous countries and mentions how Babylon was the primeval source from which ALL systems of idolatry flowed.[1] Bunsen says that the religious system of Egypt was derived from Asia, and

1. Herodotus' History, Bk. 2, p. 109.

10

"the primitive empire in Babel." In his noted work entitled NIN-EVEH AND ITS REMAINS, Layard declares that we have the united testimony of sacred and profane history that idolatry originated in the area of Babylonia—the most ancient of religious systems.[1]

Now when Rome became a world empire, it is a known fact that she assimulated into her system the gods and religions from the various pagan countries over which she ruled.[2] And since Babylon was the source of the paganism of these countries, we can see how the early religion of pagan Rome was but the Babylonish worship that had developed into various forms and under different names in the countries to which it had gone.

Bearing this in mind, we notice that it was during this time when Rome ruled the world, that the *true* saviour, Jesus Christ, was born, lived among men, died, and rose again. He then ascended into heaven, sent back the Holy Spirit, and the New Testament church was established in the earth. And what glorious days they were! One only has to read the book of Acts to see how much God blessed his people in those days. Multitudes were added to the church—the true church. Great signs and wonders were performed as God confirmed his word with signs following. True Christianity, anointed by the Holy Spirit, swept the world like a prairie fire. It encircled the mountains and crossed the oceans. It made kings to tremble and tyrants to fear. It was said of those early Christians that they had turned the world upside down!—so powerful was their message and spirit.

Before too many years had passed, however, men began to set themselves up as "lords" over God's people in place of the Holy Spirit. Instead of conquering by spiritual means and by truth —as in the early days—men began to substitute *their* ideas and *their* methods. Attempts to merge paganism into Christianity were being made even in the days when our New Testament was being written, for Paul mentioned that the "MYSTERY of iniquity" was already beginning to work. He warned that there would come a "falling away" and that m a n y would "depart from the faith giving heed to seducing spirits and doctrines of devils"—the counterfeit doctrines of the pagans! By the time that Jude wrote the book that bears his name, it was necessary for him to exhort the people to "earnestly contend for THE faith that was ONCE delivered unto the saints", for certain men had crept in and were attempting to substitute things that were not a part of the early true faith of Christ and the Apostles. (Jude 1:3, 4).

1. Vol. 2, p. 440.
2. The Legacy of Rome, p. 245.

11

Christianity came face to face with the Babylonian paganism in its various forms that had been established in the Roman Empire. The early Christians refused to have anything to do with its customs and beliefs. Much persecution resulted. Many Christians were falsely accused, thrown to the lions, burned at the stake, and in other ways tortured and martyred. But then great changes began to be made. The Emperor of Rome professed conversion. Imperial orders went forth throughout the empire that persecutions should cease. Bishops were given high honours. The church began to receive worldly recognition and power. But for all of this, a great price had to be paid!

Many compromises were made with paganism. Instead of the "church" being separate from the world, it became a part of this world system. The Emperor, showing favor, demanded a place of leadership in the church; for in paganism, emperors were believed to be gods. From here on, wholesale mixtures of paganism into Christianity were made, as all historians know.

As shocking as it may sound, the very paganism that originated in Babylon and spread to the nations, was now thoroughly mixed with Christianity, especially at Rome. This MIXTURE produced what is known today as the ROMAN CATHOLIC CHURCH —as (we believe) the pages which follow fully prove.

It is not our intention to treat lightly or to ridicule any one whose beliefs we may here disagree with. Instead, it is our desire that this book would be a call to all sincere people—regardless of church affiliation—to forsake Babylonish doctrines and concepts and turn to the Bible and to THE faith that was ONCE delivered to the saints!

CHAPTER TWO

Mother and Child Worship

NE OF THE MOST outstanding examples of how Babylonian paganism has continued to our day may be seen in the way the Romish church invented Mary worship to replace the ancient worship of the Mother Goddess of Babylon. As we mentioned in Chapter One, after the death of Nimrod, his adulterous wife gave birth to a child who she claimed was supernaturally conceived. She taught that he was a god-child; that he was Nimrod, their leader, reborn; that she and her child were divine.[1] This story was widely known in ancient Babylon and developed into a well established worship —the worship of the Mother and the Child. Numerous monuments of Babylon show the Goddess Mother Semiramis with her child Tammuz in her arms.[2] (See illustration).

Now when the people of Babylon were scattered to the various parts of the earth, they carried the worship of the Divine Mother and her god-child with them. This explains why it is that all nations in ancient times worshipped a divine Mother and god-child —in one form or another—centuries before the true saviour, our Lord Jesus, was born into this world! In the various countries where this worship spread, the Mother and Child were called by different names, due to the dividing of the languages at Babel, but the basic story remained the same.

Among the Chinese, the Mother Goddess was called Shingmoo or the "Holy Mother." She is pictured with child in arms and rays of glory around her head.[3] The ancient Germans worshipped the Virgin "Hertha" with child in arms. The Scandinavians called her "Disa" who was also pictured with a child. The Etruscans called her "Nutria" and among the Druids, the "Virgo-Paritura" was worshipped as the "Mother of God."[4] In India, she was known as

1. Two Babylons, p. 21.   3. The Heathen Religion, p. 60.
2. Encyclopedia of Religions, vol. 2, p. 398.   4. Bible Myths, p. 334.

13

Indrani, who was also represented with child in arms, as shown in the accompanying illustration.

The Babylonian Mother was known as Aphodite or Ceres to the Greeks; Nana, to the Sumerians; and as Venus or Fortuna to her devotees in the olden days of Rome, and her child was known as Jupiter.[1] The accompanying

illustration at the left, shows the Mother and child as Devaki and C r i s h n a. For ages, Isi, the "Great Goddess" and her c h i l d Iswara,

have been worshipped in India where great temples were erected for their worship.[2] In Asia, the Mother was known as Cybele and the child as Deoius. "But regardless of her name or place", says one writer, "she was the wife of Baal, the virgin queen of heaven, who bore fruit although she never conceived."[3]

When the children of Israel fell into apostasy, they too were defiled with this Mother-Goddess worship. As we read in Judges 2:13, "They forsook the LORD, and served Baal and Ashtaroth." Ashtaroth or Ashtoreth was the name by which the Goddess was known to the children of Israel. It is pitiful to think that even those who had known the true God would depart from Him and worship the heathen Mother. But this is *exactly* what they did.[4] One of the titles by which the Goddess was known among the Israelites was "the queen of heaven", as we read in Jeremiah 44:17-19. The prophet Jeremiah rebuked them for worshipping her, but they rebelled against his warning and thus brought upon themselves swift destruction from the hand of God!

In Ephesus, the Great Mother was known as Diana. The temple dedicated to her in that city was one of the Seven Wonders of the ancient world! And not only at Ephesus, but throughout all Asia and the world was the Mother-goddess worshipped (Acts 19:27).

1. Two Babylons, p. 20.
2. Ibid, p. 20.
3. Strange Sects and Curious Cults, p. 12.
4. Judges 10:6; 1 Sam. 7:3,4; 12:10; 1 Kings 11:5; 2 Kings 23:13

14

In Egypt, the Babylonian Mother was known as Isis and her child as Horus. Nothing is more common on the religious monuments of Egypt than the infant Horus seated on the lap of his mother (as seen in the accompanying drawing).

The worship of the Mother and Child was also known in England in olden times, for in 1747, a religious monument was found at Oxford, of pagan origin, on which is exhibited a female nursing an infant. "Thus we see," says the historian, "that the Virgin and child were worshipped in pagan times from China to Britain... and even in Mexico the 'Mother and child' were worshipped."[1]

This false worship, having spread from Babylon to the various nations, in different names and forms, finally became established at Rome and throughout the Roman Empire. Says a noted writer of this period: "The worship of the Great Mother... was very popular under the Roman Empire. Inscriptions prove that the two (the Mother and the Child) received divine honours... not only in Italy and especially at Rome, but also in the provinces, particularly in Africa, Spain, Portugal, France, Germany, and Bulgaria."[2]

Now it was during this period when the worship of the Divine Mother was very prominent that the saviour, our Lord Jesus Christ, founded the *true* New Testament church. And what a glorious church it was in those early days! By the third and fourth centuries, however, what was known as the "church" greatly departed from the original faith, falling into that great apostasy about which the apostles had warned. When this "falling away" came, much paganism was mixed with Christianity. Unconverted pagans were taken into the professing church and in numerous instances were allowed to continue many of their pagan rites and customs—usually with a few reservations or changes to make these pagan beliefs appear more similar to some Christian doctrine.

One of the best examples of such a carry over from paganism may be seen in the way the professing church allowed the pagans to continue their worship of the Great Mother—only in a slightly different form and with a new name! You see, many pagans had

1. Bible Myths, p. 334.
2. The Golden Bough, Vol. 1, p. 356.

been drawn to Christianity, but so strong in their mind was the adoration for the Mother-goddess, that they did not want to forsake her. Compromising church leaders saw that if they could find some similarity in Christianity with the Mother-goddess worship of the pagans, they could increase their numbers by bringing many pagans into their fold. But who could they use to replace the Great Mother of paganism? Of course Mary, the Mother of Jesus was the most logical person for them to choose. Why then couldn't they allow the pagans to *continue* their prayers and devotion to the Goddess, but call her by the name of Mary instead of the former names by which she was known? This would give the pagan worship of the Mother the *appearance* of Christianity, and in this way, both sides could be pleased—as it were —and drawn into the Romish system.

And this is exactly what happened! Little by little, the worship and doctrines that had been associated with the pagan Mother came to be applied to Mary. Thus the pagan worship of the "Mother" continued — hiding now right within the professing church!

It is evident that this Mary-worship was not the worship of Mary at all, but a continuation of the old pagan worship of the pagan Mother. For while Mary, the mother of Jesus, was a fine, dedicated, and godly woman—especially chosen to bear the body of our saviour—yet never was she considered as a DIVINE person or a goddess by the early true church. None of the Apostles or even the Lord Jesus himself ever hinted at the idea of Mary worship. As the ENCYCLOPEDIA BRITANNICA states, during the first centuries of the church, no emphasis was placed upon Mary whatsoever.[1] It was not until the time of Constantine—the early part of the fourth century—that anyone began to look to Mary as a goddess. But even at this period, such worship was frowned upon by the church, as is evident by the words of Epiphanius who denounced certain women of Thrace, Arabia, and elsewhere, for worshipping Mary as an actual goddess and offering cakes at her shrine. Yet, within just a few more years, Mary worship was not only condoned by what is known today as the Catholic Church, but it became one of her main doctrines—as it is to this day.

Since Rome had long been a center for the worship of the Goddess of paganism, we need not be surprised that this was one of the first places that Mary worship became established within the "Church", a fact that plainly reveals that Mary worship was the direct result of pagan influence!

1. Vol. 14, p. 309.

16

Another city where the ancient pagan Mother worship was very popular was Ephesus; and here too, attempts were made to merge it into Christianity. In Ephesus, from primitive times, the Mother Goddess had been called Diana. (Acts 19). Here, the pagans had worshipped her as the goddess of Virginity and Motherhood.[1] She was said to represent the generative powers of nature and so was pictured with many breasts. A tower shaped crown, a symbol of the tower of Babel, adorned her head. (See illustration.)

When beliefs are held by a people for centuries, they are not easily forsaken. So church leaders at Ephesus — when the falling away came — also reasoned that if they would let the pagans continue their old worship of the Great Mother, they could bring them into the "church." So here too, at Ephesus, the Mother Goddess worship was mixed into Christianity, the name of Mary being substituted in the place of the name Diana. The pagans continued to pray to the Mother Goddess, they kept their idols of her, and the professing church allowed them to worship her along with Christ. But such a mixture was not God's way of gaining "converts"!

When Paul had come to Ephesus in earlier days, no compromise was made with paganism. People were *truly* converted in those days and destroyed their idols of the Mother-goddess (Acts 19:24-27). How tragic that this church in later centuries compromised and even adopted the abominable Mother-goddess worship —hiding it under a cloak of professing Christianity! And finally, when the worship of Mary was made an official doctrine of the Catholic church in 431 A. D. , in what city did it take place? It was at the Council of *Ephesus* —the city of the pagan Mother Diana! The pagan influence in such a decision is apparent.

Another stronghold for the worship of the Great Mother of heathenism was Alexandria, Egypt. Here she was known by the

1. Fausset's Bible Encyclopedia, p. 484.

name Isis. As Christianity spread to Alexandria, similar compromises were made as had been made at Ephesus and Rome. The pagan Mother worship was skillfully injected into "Christianity" by the church theologians of this city. Now the very fact that it was in cities like Alexandria, Ephesus, and Rome, where the worship of the pagan Mother was first mixed into Christian worship, clearly shows how such was the direct continuation of the old paganism.

Further proof that Mary-worship is but the outgrowth of the old popular worship of the Pagan Mother Goddess, may be seen in the TITLES that are ascribed to her. Let us notice how the pagan titles by which the Mother Goddess was known were smoothly transferred to Mary, and much of the old worship continued!

For example, Mary is often called "THE MADONNA." But such a title has absolutely nothing to do with Mary, the mother of Jesus! Instead, this expression is the translation of one of the titles by which the Babylonian Goddess was known! In deified form, Nimrod came to be known as Baal. The title of his wife, the female divinity, would be the equivalent of Baalti. In English, this word means "My Lady"; in Latin, "Mea Domina", and in Italian, it is corrupted into the well-known *"Madonna"!* [1]

Among the Phoenicians, the Mother Goddess was known as "The Lady of the Sea" [2] and even this title is applied to Mary — though there is no connection between Mary and the sea whatsoever!

The scriptures make it plain that there is ONE mediator between God and men, the man Christ Jesus (1 Tim. 2:5). Yet Roman Catholicism teaches that Mary is also a "mediator." And therefore, prayers to her form a very important part of Catholic worship. But how was it that Mary came to be looked upon as a mediator? Again the influence of paganism is obvious. You see, the Mother Goddess of Babylon bore as one of her names, "Mylitta", that is, "The Mediatrix." And so this too passed into the apostate church which to this day speaks of Mary as the Mediatrix or Mediator!

Another title that was borrowed from paganism and applied to Mary is "the queen of heaven." But Mary, the mother of Jesus, is *not* the queen of heaven, for the "queen of heaven" was a title of the pagan Mother-goddess that was worshipped centuries before Mary was ever born! Yes, way back in the days of Jeremiah, the people were worshipping the "Queen of heaven" and practicing rites that were sacred to her. As we read in Jeremiah 7:18-20: "The children gather wood, and the fathers kindle the fire, and

1. Two Babylons, p. 20.
2. Harper's Bible Dictionary, p. 47.

18

the women knead their dough, to make cakes to the queen of heaven." And in this connection, it is interesting to note that right down to modern times at Paphos, in Cyprus, the women made offerings to the Virgin Mary as Queen of heaven, in the ruins of the ancient Temple of Astarte.[1]

As we have seen, the name of the Mother-goddess in Egypt was Isis and her son's name was Horus. Now one of the titles by which Isis was known was the "Mother of God." Later this same title was applied to Mary by the theologians of Alexandria.[2] This again was obviously an attempt to make Christianity appear similar to the ancient paganism with its Mother-goddess worship. Now we know that Mary was the mother of Jesus, but *only* in the sense of his human nature, his humanity. The Catholic title and the original meaning of the title, however, went beyond this. It attached a glorified position to the MOTHER and in much the same way, Roman Catholics are taught to think of Mary today!

The worship of Isis, the Egyptian form of the Babylonian Mother Goddess, was not limited to Egypt. It was introduced into Rome about 80 B.C. when Sulla founded an Isiac college there. And to show to what extent that paganism was mixed with "Christianity" at Rome, we need only to mention the fact that Isis, the pagan "Mother of God", was worshipped in a shrine that "stood on the Vatican Hill where now stands St. Peter's, the centre of the church which worships the 'Mother of God' in just that capacity"![3]

And so the titles "queen of heaven", "Lady of the Sea", "Mediatrix", "Madonna", "Mother of God", and others—all of which were the titles of the *pagan* Mother-Goddess—were, little by little, applied to Mary. Such titles plainly show that the SUPPOSED worship of Mary today is in reality the continuation of the Goddess worship of pagan times. But there is further proof of this that can be seen in the way that Mary came to be represented in the *art* of the fallen church:

So firmly written in the paganistic mind was the image of the Mother Goddess with child in her arms, that when the days of the great falling away came, "the ancient portrait of Isis and the child Horus was ultimately accepted not only in popular opinion, but by formal episcopal sanction, as the portrait of the Virgin and her child."[4] Representations of Isis and her child were often enclosed in a framework of flowers. This practice too was applied to Mary who is often pictured the same way, as those who have studied Medieval Art well know.

The Egyptian goddess Isis was often represented as standing

1. The Paganism in Our Christianity, p. 133.   4. Man and His Gods, p. 216
2. Ibid, p. 130.
3. Ibid, p. 128-9.   19

on the *Crescent moon* with *twelve* stars surrounding her head.[1] Even this was adopted and applied to Mary, for in almost every Roman Catholic church on the continent of Europe may be seen pictures of Mary exactly the same way! The accompanying illustration (as seen in the OFFICIAL BALTIMORE CATECHISM) pictures Mary with the twelve stars circling her head and the crescent moon under her feet!

To satisfy the superstitious minds of the heathen, leaders of the falling away attempted to make Mary appear similar to the goddess of paganism and exalt her to a divine plane to compete with the pagan Mother. And even as the pagans had *statues* of the Goddess, so likewise, statues were made of "Mary"—even though the scriptures forbid such a practice! In some cases, the VERY SAME statues that had been worshipped as Isis (with her child), were simply renamed as Mary and the Christ child—and the old worship continued! "When Christianity triumphed", says one writer, "these paintings and figures became those of the Madonna and child without any break in continuity: No archaeologist, in fact, can now tell whether some of these objects represent the one or the other."[2]

All of this shows how far apostate leaders went in their attempt to merge paganism with Christianity. Many of these renamed figures are crowned and adorned with jewels—in exactly the same way as the images of the Hindoo and Egyptian Virgins. Now Mary, the mother of Jesus was not rich, but poor. From where then came the jewels and the crowns seen on these statues that are supposedly of her? Obviously such representations are not Christian, but are of a pre-Christian origin instead!

And so by compromises—some very obvious, others more hidden—the worship of the ancient Mother of the pagans was continued within the "church", the church of the falling away, with the name of Mary being substituted in place of the old names. And this slight change has deceived the world!

1. Kenrick's Egypt, vol. 1, p. 425; Isis Unveiled, p. 49.
2. The Paganism in Our Christianity, p. 129.

20

CHAPTER THREE
Mary Worship 2-9-10

PERHAPS THE MOST outstanding proof that Mary worship is a continuation of the old pagan worship (and not of Mary at all) may be seen from the fact that in pagan religion, the MOTHER was worshipped as much or more than her son! Here then is an outstanding clue to help us solve the Mystery of Babylon today! True Christianity teaches that the Lord Jesus—and HE alone—is the way, the truth, and the life; that only HE can for-give sin; that only HE, of all earth's creatures, has ever lived a life that was never stained with wrong; and HE is to be worshipped —NEVER HIS MOTHER. But Roman Catholicism—showing the influence that paganism has had in its developement—exalts the MOTHER also! In fact, in many ways the Mother is exalted *more* than the Son.

Of course, some might try to deny that the Catholic church attributes such a divine position to Mary. But one can travel the world over, and whether in a massive Cathedral or in a village chapel, the statue of Mary will occupy the most prominent position. In reciting the Rosary prayers, the "Hail Mary" is repeated nine times as often as the "Lord's prayer." Say what one will, Mary is the most important name in Catholicism. In a very similar way as the ancient Babylonians glorified their Mother-goddess, so do those in Modern Babylon today—only they use the name Mary instead of the former names by which the goddess was known.

Catholics are taught that the reason for praying to Mary is that she can take the petition to her Son, Jesus; and since she is his MOTHER, he will answer the request for her sake. The inference is that Mary is more compassionate, understanding, and merci-ful than her son, the Lord Jesus. Certainly such a position is blasphemous and utterly contrary to the scriptures! Yet this idea is often repeated in Catholic writings.

One noted Roman Catholic writer, Alphonsus Liguori, wrote at length telling how much more effectual prayers are that are addressed to Mary rather than to Christ. And that his writings

21

carried Catholic approval is evident from the fact that he was canonized as a "saint" by Pope Gregory XIV in 1839 and was declared a "doctor" of the Catholic church by Pope Pius IX.

In one portion of his writings, Ligouri describes an imaginary scene in which a sinful man sees two ladders hanging from heaven. Mary is at the top of one; Jesus at the top of the other. When the sinner tries to climb the one ladder, he sees the angry face of Christ and falls defeated. But when he climbs Mary's ladder, he ascends easily and is openly welcomed by Mary who brings him into heaven and presents him to Christ! Then all is well. The story is supposed to show how much easier and more effective it is to go to Christ through Mary.[1]

This same Catholic writer said that the sinner who ventures to come directly to Christ may come with dread of his wrath. But if he will pray to the *Virgin*, she will only have to "show" that son "the breasts that gave him suck" and his wrath will be immediately appeased![2] Certainly such a heathenistic idea is contrary to the scriptures. In fact, the scriptures give us an illustration that fully refutes such a position: "Blessed is the womb that bare thee", a woman once said to Jesus, "and the paps that thou has sucked!" But Jesus answered, "Yea, rather blessed are they that hear the word of God and keep it"(Luke 11:27, 28).

Obviously then the idea that Jesus would be persuaded to answer a prayer because Mary shows him the breasts that he had sucked, is contrary to the scriptures. But such ideas about the breasts, on the other hand, were not foreign to the worshippers of the pagan Mother-goddess. Idols of the Goddess have been unearthed which often show her breasts extremely out of proportion to her body. Or, as in the case of Diana, to symbolize her "fertility", she is pictured with as many as one hundred breasts!

Catholicism has further attempted to exalt Mary to a glorified position as evidenced by the doctrine of the *"Immaculate conception."* Now such a teaching, it would seem, is only a further effort to make Mary more closely resemble the Goddess of paganism, for in the old myths, the goddess was also believed to have had a supernatural conception! These old fable stories varied, but all told of supernatural happenings in connection with her entrance into the world. They taught that she was superior to ordinary mortals; that she was divine. And so, little by little, to make the teachings about Mary harmonize with the pagan teachings, it was necessary to teach that Mary's entrance into this world was supernatural also!

1. Roman Catholicism, p. 147.
2. Two Babylons, p. 158.

22

The supernatural element in the Roman Catholic teaching about Mary is that she was born without the stain of original sin. But of such a birth the scriptures are silent. Concerning Mary, the Bible *does* say that she was a chosen vessel of the Lord; she was a Godly and virtuous woman—a *virgin*—but she was as much a HUMAN as you or I. And as a human, she was a member of Adam's family—a *fallen* family. As the scriptures declare, "ALL have sinned and come short of the glory of God", and the only exception to this is the Lord Jesus himself. Like everyone else, Mary needed a saviour! And this she plainly admitted when she said: "And my spirit hath rejoiced in God my SAVIOUR"(Lk. 1:47).

Obviously if Mary needed a saviour, then she was not a saviour herself. If she needed a saviour, then she needed to be saved, forgiven, and redeemed—even as others. The fact is: Our Lord's divinity did not depend on his Mother being some type of exalted, super-human person. No; instead he was divine because he was the only begotten *Son of God*. His divinity came from his Heavenly Father.

Let us understand that it was JESUS that was born of a supernatural conception, not his mother! The idea that Mary was superior to other human beings was utterly refuted by Jesus Himself! One day while he was preaching, "his mother and his brethren stood without, desiring to speak with him." Then someone said, "Behold thy mother and thy brethren stand without, desiring to speak with thee." But Jesus answered: "Who is my mother? and who are my brethren? And stretching forth his hand toward his disciples, he said: "Behold my mother and my brethren! For WHOSOEVER shall do the will of my Father which is in heaven, the same is my brother, and sister, and MOTHER" (Matt. 12:46-50). Plainly enough then, if we serve the Lord—if we do his will—then we are on the same level with Mary or any other Christian. Certainly this oneness in Christ shows an EQUALITY in the sight of God and refutes the idea that Mary was a super-human person.

However, Romanism had adopted from paganism the idea of praying to the Divine Mother and so it *had* to teach that Mary was a superhuman person—how else could she hear so many prayers as those that are addressed to her? Each day Catholics the world over recite the Hail Mary, the Rosary, the Angelus, the Litanies of the Blessed Virgin, and others. Multiplying the number of these prayers, times the number of Catholics that recite these prayers each day, it has been figured that Mary would have to listen to 46,296 petitions a *second* —and this is a conservative estimate!

23

Obviously, no one could do this but God himself. Nevertheless, Catholics believe that Mary hears all of these prayers; and so, of necessity, they have had to exalt her to the Divine level—scriptural or not!

Attempting to justify such undue exaltation of Mary, Catholic leaders have sought for a *scriptural* basis for the belief. The words of Gabriel to Mary, "Blessed art thou among women"(Lk. 1:28) have often been referred to in this connection. Now most assuredly the words of Gabriel indicate that Mary was chosen of the Lord. But simply because she was "blessed among women" would not make her a *divine* person, for 1300 years before, a similar blessing was pronounced upon Jael, of whom it was said: "Blessed above women shall Jael the wife of Heber the Kenite be ..."(Judges 5:24). It seems quite evident then that the words which tell us Mary was "blessed among women" do not prove that we should worship her, pray to her, or think of her as a goddess.

Before Pentecost, Mary was gathered with the other disciples waiting for the promise of the Holy Spirit. We read that the apostles "all continued with one accord in prayer and supplication, with the women, and MARY the mother of Jesus, and his brethren" (Acts 1:14). Certainly the scriptures do not say that the disciples were praying to Mary, were worshipping her, or that she even took any prominent position. But typical of Catholic ideas concerning Mary, the accompanying illustration (as seen in the Catholic Catechism books [1]) attempts to give to Mary a *central* position. But as all students of the Bible know, the disciples were

not looking to Mary on that occasion, they were looking to their resurrected and ascended CHRIST to outpour on them the gift of the Holy Spirit! We notice also in the drawing that not only are
1. Official Baltimore Catechism, Number 2, (Lesson 11).

24

the disciples pictured as looking to Mary, but even the Holy Spirit (as a dove) is seen hovering over her! However, as far as the scriptural account is concerned, the only one upon whom the Spirit in this form ever descended was Jesus Himself—not his mother! On the other hand—and this sounds almost incredible—but the pagan Virgin Goddess under the name of Juno was often represented with a dove on her head, as was also Astarte, Cybele, and Isis![1] And so the pagan influence in such pictures seems apparent.

Further attempts to glorify Mary—to exalt her to a position the scriptures nowhere assign to her—may be seen in the Catholic doctrine known as the PERPETUAL VIRGINITY of Mary. This is the teaching that Mary remained a virgin throughout her life. But *never* was this doctrine taught by Christ or the Apostles. As the ENCYCLOPEDIA BRITANNICA explains, the doctrine of the perpetual virginity of Mary was not taught until about three hundred years AFTER our Lord's return to heaven! It was not until the meetings of the Council of Chalcedon in 451 that this fabulous quality gained the official recognition of Rome.[2]

Quite contrary to Catholic teachings, however, the scriptures plainly show that Mary did NOT remain a virgin throughout her life. The scriptures teach that our Lord Jesus was born to the virgin Mary—virgin born—supernaturally born (Matt. 1:23). We *most assuredly* believe in the virgin birth of Christ! But, *after* Jesus was born, Mary gave birth to other children—the natural offspring of her union with Joseph, her husband:

In Matthew 1:25, we read that Jesus was Mary's "FIRSTBORN" son. The Bible does not say that Mary brought forth her ONLY child; it says, instead, that Jesus was her firstborn child. Now the fact that Jesus was her "firstborn" child, would certainly infer that she later had a second-born child, possibly a third-born child, etc.

But beyond this line of reasoning, the scriptures leave no room for doubt as to the fact that Mary did have other children after Jesus was born. Their names are listed in the Bible as follows: James, Joses, Simon, and Judas (Matt. 13:55). Besides these four brothers, the passage goes on to mention the sisters of Jesus. The people of Nazareth said: "And his sisters, are they not *all* with us?"(verse 56). The word "sisters" is in the plural, so we know that Jesus had at least two sisters. But a still closer look at the passage indicates that Jesus not only had two sisters, but at least three or more! Notice that the verse speaks of "all" his

1. Doane, p. 357.
2. Vol. 14, p. 999.

25

sisters. Usually if we are referring to only two people, we would say "both" of them, not "all" of them. That the expression refers to at least three sisters is definitely implied. If we then figure three sisters and four brothers, half-brothers and half-sisters to Jesus, this would make Mary the mother of eight children all together.

The Lord Jesus was born to Mary supernaturally—born of virgin birth. The remaining seven children that were born to her were born by natural birth, children that Mary conceived from her husband Joseph. But the Catholic position is that Joseph kept Mary as a virgin all of their married life. However, she remained a virgin—according to the scriptures—only until after Jesus was born. "Joseph...knew her not till she had brought forth her firstborn son: and He called his name JESUS"(Matt. 1:25). Joseph "knew her not" until after Jesus was born, but after that, Mary and Joseph did come together as husband and wife and children were born to them—as we have seen. Considering then how the scriptures plainly teach these things, is not the doctrine of the "perpetual virginity" of Mary utterly erroneous?

During the times of the great falling away, to more closely identify Mary with the Mother Goddess that the nations had been worshipping for centuries, men also began to teach that Mary's body never saw corruption, that she bodily ascended into heaven, and that she is there today as the "queen of heaven", to receive worship and prayers! It was not until this present century, however, that the doctrine of the Assumption of Mary was officially proclaimed as a doctrine of the Roman Catholic church. It was in 1951 that Pope Pius XII proclaimed that Mary's body saw no corruption, but was taken to heaven. Obviously then, the doctrine of the Assumption of the Virgin was not a part of New Testament doctrine.

The following words of St.Bernard sum up the Catholic position in this connection: "On the third day after Mary's death, when the apostles gathered around her tomb, they found it empty. The sacred body had been carried up to the Celestial Paradise...the grave had no power over one who was immaculate...But it was not enough that Mary should be received into heaven. She was to be no ordinary citizen...she had a dignity beyond the reach even of the highest of the archangels. Mary was to be crowned Queen of Heaven by the eternal Father: she was to have a throne at her Son's right hand...Now day by day, hour by hour, she is praying for us, obtaining graces for us, preserving us from danger, shielding us from temptation, showering down blessings upon us..."

26

Now the worship of Mary—in its entirety—is based upon this belief that she bodily ascended into heaven. But the Bible says absolutely nothing about the so-called Assumption of Mary. On the other hand, John 3:13 says: "No man hath ascended up to heaven, but he that came down from heaven, even the Son of man which is in heaven"—our Lord Jesus Christ. HE is the one that is at God's right hand, HE is the one that is our mediator, HE is the one that showers down blessings upon us—not his mother!

The Bible nowhere tells us to pray to a woman—Mary or anyone else. Such false worship is repeatedly forbidden in the Bible. True prayers must be addressed to our Lord himself. "For there is one God, and one mediator between God and men, the man Christ Jesus"(1 Tim. 2:5). The very idea of "praying to Mary" as a "mediator", as the "queen of heaven", is but paganism disguised with the name Mary.

Closely connected with the prayers that are prayed to "Mary" is the Rosary, which, as we shall see is equally pagan in origin: As an instrument, the rosary is a chain with fifteen sets of small beads, each set marked off by one large bead. The ends of this chain are joined by a medal bearing the imprint of Mary. From this hangs a short chain at the end of which is a crucifix, a cross with a dead saviour hanging on it.

The beads on the rosary are for counting prayers, prayers that are repeated over and over. Such an instrument, as is well known, is a very important part of Catholic worship. But like so many things in the Catholic church, the rosary is not a Christian instrument, but a pagan invention. Long before there ever was a Catholic church, the rosary was in common use in almost every pagan nation!

A medal has been found at Citium, in Cyprus, colonized by the Phoenicians, which bears a circle of beads resembling a rosary. This rosary was used in the worship of Astarte, the Mother Goddess, about 800 B.C. !¹ This same "rosary" is seen on some of the early Phoenician coins.

The Brahmans have from early times used rosaries with tens and hundreds of beads. The worshippers of Vishnu give their children rosaries of 108 beads. A similar rosary is used by millions of Buddhists in India and Tibet.² The Moslem con-

1. The Cross in Tradition, History, and Art, p. 21.
2. Encyclopedia of Religions, Vol. 3, p. 203.

stantly fingers the Tasbih rosary with 99 beads for the 99 names of Allah.[1] The worshipper of Siva has a rosary upon which he rehearses, if possible, all the 1008 names of his god.[2]

When Catholic missionaries first visited India, Japan, and Mexico—places that had never heard of Christ—they were shocked to find rosaries already in use by pagans! The demon-worshippers of Thibet and China use rosaries in their rituals. Rosaries are often mentioned in the sacred books of the Hindoos.[3] The rosary was used in Asiatic Greece and such was the purpose (according to Hislop) of the beads that are seen on the statue of Diana.[4] Literature of the second and third centuries BEFORE the Christian era, mentions the use of rosaries among various heathen religions. And not only was the rosary in evidence in all these countries and among these religions that we have mentioned, but such was also used in the days of pagan ROME! In Rome, the necklaces worn by the women were not merely for ornamental reasons—but for the REMEMBERANCE of prayers in their heathenistic religion—the word necklace, "Monile", meaning "Remembrancer."[5]

That the rosary instrument was used in pre-Christian times and by non-Christian religions none can deny. Even the CATHOLIC ENCYCLOPEDIA says: "In almost all countries, then, we meet with something in the nature of prayer-counters or rosary-beads."

However, neither Christ or the Apostles ever taught us to use an instrument to count our prayers! Memorizing a prayer, then repeating it over and over, while we count rosary beads, actually becomes more of a "memory test" than a spontaneous expression of prayer from the heart. Considering that its use is without scriptural support and that its origin was among heathen tribes, the rosary is but another example of how paganism was mixed into the Catholic religion.

The most oft-repeated prayer and the main prayer of the rosary is the "Hail Mary" which is as follows: "Hail Mary, full of grace, the Lord is with thee; Blessed art thou among women, and blessed is the fruit of thy womb, Jesus. Holy Mary, Mother of God, pray for us sinners, now and at the hour of death, Amen."

In all, reciting the complete rosary takes about 15 minutes. It involves repeating the Hail Mary 53 times, the Lord's prayer 6 times, 5 mysteries, 5 meditations on the Mysteries, 5 glory Be's and one repeating of the Apostles' Creed(so-called). Now let us notice where the emphasis is placed. Which prayer is re-

1. Ibid, p.205.   4. Two Babylons, p.187.
2. Ibid, p.203.   5. Ibid, p.188.
3. Doane, p.344.

peated the most? It is the prayer to Mary! In fact, the Hail Mary prayer is repeated almost NINE TIMES as often as the Lord's prayer. But we ask: is a prayer composed by men and directed to Mary nine times as important or effective as the prayer taught by Jesus and directed to God himself? Such an extreme emphasis on the "MOTHER" again plainly shows the mixture of paganism into the system of Rome!

Repeating a prayer over and over is shown in the Bible to be a practice of the heathen! For example, repetitious prayers were used in connection with the Diana worship at Ephesus. These prayers consisted of a short religious phrase repeated over and over, as we read in Acts 19:34. In this passage, the worshippers of the Mother Goddess "all with one voice about the space of two hours cried out, Great is Diana of the Ephesians." They kept saying this over and over. And even as those worshippers of Diana used repetitious phrases in their worship, even so today, the same type of unscriptural praying continues in the Catholic church—now supposedly to Mary!

But Jesus Christ was directly opposed to the practice of repeat- ⊓ ing a prayer over and over—and plainly said so! "When ye pray", he declared, "use not vain repetitions, as the heathen do; for they think that they shall be heard for their much speaking. Be not ye therefore like unto them: for your Father knoweth what things ye have need of before ye ask him"(Matt. 6:7-13). In this passage, our Lord in no uncertain terms told us NOT to pray a little pray- ▽ er over and over. Jesus said it was heathenistic. Will we believe Him and will we obey?

Of all the rosary prayers, the only one that is taken directly from the Bible is "The Lord's Prayer." But even this prayer was not to be repeated over and over, for after our Lord told us not to use repetitions as the heathen do, in the very next verse, he said: "After this manner therefore pray ye: Our Father which art in heaven..." and he gave the disciples this sample prayer. In the very same passage in which he warned of vain repetition, the Lord Jesus gave this prayer as an OPPOSITE to the heathen type of prayer. And yet, in direct disobedience to the scriptures, Catholics are taught to repeat this prayer over and over. And if even the "Lord's Prayer" was not to be repeated over and over, how much less should we repeat over and over a little man-made ▽ prayer to Mary, his human mother?

CHAPTER FOUR

Saints, Saints' Days, and Symbols

IN ADDITION TO the prayers and devotions that are directed to "Mary", Roman Catholics also honour and pray to various "saints." Now these saints—according to the Catholic position— are martyrs or other notable people of the "church" who have died and whom the Popes have pronounced saints. In this chapter we shall see the astounding proof, however, that the idea of praying to saints was but a continuation of the old devotion that the pagans gave to the gods and goddesses of their religion from the earliest times! But before we notice this evidence, let us first look into the Holy Scriptures and see what the Bible teaches concerning saints.

According to the Bible, ALL true Christians are saints! There is certainly no indication that a person becomes a saint after he is dead. And it is not a pope that makes anyone a saint. This is *God's* business! In the scriptures, saints are *living* people, never the dead. For example, when Paul wrote to the Ephesians, his letter was addressed: "To the saints that are at Ephesus"(Eph. 1:1). The book of Philippians was written "to all the saints that are at Philippi"(Phil. 1:1). The early Christians in the church at Rome were called saints (Rom. 1:7; 16:15) as were also those Christians who lived at Corinth (1 Cor. 1:2; 2 Cor. 1:1).

Therefore, if we want a "saint" to pray for us, we should find a Christian and let him join us in prayer. But if we try to contact people that have died, what else could it be but a form of spiritism? Repeatedly the Bible condemns all attempts to commune with the dead, for such is actually demonism (see Isaiah 8:19, 20). Yet many recite the "Apostles' Creed" that says: "We believe... in the communion of saints" and believe that such has reference not only to the living, but to the "departed" as well— "a mutual sharing in help, satisfaction, prayer, and other good works, a mutual communication" (New Catholic Encyclopedia,

Vol. 4, page 41.)

But the scriptures are against the idea of the living being blessed or benefited by prayers to or through those who have already died. Such teachings are completely foreign to the Bible. How then did these things enter into the Romish Church?

Again we look back to the "Mother" of false religion—Babylon. Here, from the earliest times we find that the people prayed to and honoured a plurality of gods. In fact, the Babylonian system developed until it had some 5,000 gods and goddesses.[1] And in much the same way as Catholics believe about their "saints", the Babylonians believed that their gods and goddesses had at one time been living heros on earth, but were now on a higher plane. [2] "Every month and every day of the month was under the protection of a particular divinity."[3] Some of these gods and goddesses were associated with various seasons, others with certain events in life, and other were connected with various occupations.

From Babylon—like the worship of the Great Mother—the worship of these "gods" spread to every nation. The Buddhists in China, to cite one of many examples that could be given, have their "worship of various deities, as the goddess of sailors, the god of war, the gods of special neighborhoods or occupations."[4]

When Rome conquered the world, this system of gods and goddesses was absorbed in like manner into the religion of pagan Rome. Brighit, for example, was goddess of smiths and poetry. Juno Regina was the goddess of womanhood, marriage, and maternity; Minerva was the goddess of schools—of wisdom, handicrafts, and musicians; Venus was the goddess of sexual love and birth; Vesta was the goddess of bakers and sacred fires; Hercules was the god of joy and wine; Mercury was the patron deity of merchants, orators, and thieves; Ops, was the goddess of wealth; Bellona was the goddess of war; the pagan gods Castor and Pollux were the protectors of Rome and of travelers at sea; Apollo was the god of medicine and health; Cronus was the guardian of oaths; and Janus was the god of doors and gates.[5]

And so the Babylonish idea of gods and goddesses associated with various days and events in life became established in pagan Rome. Then later when the great falling away came, this very same practice was merged into the "church" at Rome. Since new converts from paganism were reluctant to part with their "gods" unless they could find some satisfactory counterpart in Christ-

1. In the Beginnings, p. 65.
2. Encyclopedia of Religions, Vol. 2, p. 78.
3. The Historians' History of the World, Vol. 1, p. 518.
4. The Story of the World's Worship, p. 621.
5. Durant, Vol. 3, p. 61-63; World's Worship, p. 179; Life in the Roman World, p. 377;

31

ianity—these old gods and goddesses were simply renamed and called "saints." And even as the pagans had believed in divinities associated with various *occupations*—each with its special *day*—so this *same* belief continued and is a very important part of the Catholic church to this day! This is seen in the following table of Catholic saints, the occupations they are associated with, and their special days:

Actors	St. Genesius	August 25
Architects	St. Thomas	December 21
Astronomers	St. Cominic	August 4
Athletes	St. Sebastain	January 20
Aviators	Our Lady of Loreto	December 10
Bakers	St. Elizabeth	November 19
Bankers	St. Matthew	September 21
Barbers	S. S. Cosmas & Damian	September 27
Beggars	St. Alexius	July 17
Book Sellers	St. John of God	March 8
Bricklayers	St. Steven	December 26
Builders	St. Vincent Ferrer	April 5
Butchers	St. Hadrian	September 28
Cab drivers	St. Fiarce	August 30
Candle-makers	St. Bernard	August 20
Comedians	St. Vitus	June 15
Cooks	St. Martha	July 29
Dentists	St. Appollonia	February 9
Doctors	St. Luke	October 18
Editors	St. John Bosco	January 31
Fishermen	St. Andrew	November 30
Florists	St. Dorothy	February 6
Grocers	St. Michael	September 29
Hat makers	St. James	May 11
Housekeepers	St. Anne	July 26
Hunters	St. Huber	November 3
Laborers	St. James the Greater	July 25
Lawyers	St. Ives	May 19
Librarians	St. Jerome	September 30
Merchants	St. Francis of Assisi	October 4
Miners	St. Barbara	December 4
Musicians	St. Cecilia	November 22
Notaries	St. Mark the Evang.	April 25

Nurses	St. Cathrine	April 30
Painters	St. Luke	October 18
Pharmacists	St. Gemma Galgani	April 11
Plasterers	St. Bartholomew	August 24
Policemen	St. Michael	September 29
Postal workers	St. Gabriel	March 24
Printers	St. John of God	March 8
Sailors	St. Brendan	May 16
Scientists	St. Albert	November 15
Shoemakers	St. Crispan	September 29
Singers	St. Gregory	March 12
Steel workers	St. Eliguis	December 1
Stenographers	St. Genesius	August 25
Students	St. Thomas Aquinas	March 7
Surgeons	S.S. Cosmas & Damian	September 27
Tailors	St. Boniface of Credtion	June 5
Tax Collectors	St. Matthew	September 21
Teachers	St. Gregory the Great	March 12

The accompanying illustration shows the way Catholic calendars designate certain of their "saints" for certain days (as we have mentioned). In addition to the "saints" that are dedicated to the

various occupations, Catholics are taught to pray to the following "saints" for help in connection with these *afflictions*:

Arthritis	St. James	Epilepsy, nerves	St. Vitus
Bite of dogs	St. Hubert	Fever	St. George
Bite of snakes	St. Hilary	Foot diseases	St. Victor
Blindness	St. Raphael	Gall stones	St. Liberius
Cancer	St. Peregrine	Gout	St. Andrew
Cramps	St. Murice	Headaches	St. Denis
Deafness	St. Cadoc	Heart trouble	St. John of God
Disease of breast	St. Agatha	Insanity	St. Dympna
Disease of eyes	St. Lucy	Skin disease	St. Roch
Disease of throat	St. Blase	Sterility	St. Giles

33

The Catholic church also has "saints" for the following:

Barren women	St. Anthony	Old maids	St. Andrew
Beer drinkers	St. Nicholas	Poor	St. Lawrence
Children	St. Dominic	Pregnant women	St. Gerard
Domestic animals	St. Anthony A.	Television	St. Clare
Emigrants	St. Francis	Temptation	St. Syriacus
Family troubles	St. Eustachius	To apprehend thieves	St. Gervase
Fire	St. Lawrence	To have children	St. Felicitas
Floods	St. Columban	To obtain a husband	St. Joseph
Lightning storms	St. Barbara	To obtain a wife	St. Anne
Lovers	St. Raphael	To find lost articles	St. Anthony

Beyond all possibility of doubt, the Catholic system of patron saints is nothing more nor less than a continuation of the ancient heathen beliefs in gods devoted to days, occupations, and the various needs of human life. Since the worship of saints is really a continuation of these false gods, Romanism is found guilty of worshipping "other gods" beside the true GOD! —a practice that is repeatedly condemned in the scriptures.

This method of substituting "saints" in the place of the pagan "gods" became so popular that by the 10th Century, 25,000 "saints" had been canonized by the Roman Catholic church. By mixing the two religions together, both the pagans and the professing Christians swelled the numbers of the Romish system.

However, to make such an apparent mixture appear less obvious, when it was possible, the leaders of Romanism would substitute a Christian sounding name that was SIMILAR to the name of the old pagan god it replaced! For example, the goddess Victoria of the Basses-Alpes was renamed as St. Victoire! The pagan god Osiris was renamed as St. Onuphris, Cheron as St. Ceraunos, Artemis as St. Artemidos, Dionysus as St. Dionysus, Apollo as St. Apolinaris, and Mars as St. Martine![1]

The pagan Goddess Brighit (regarded as the daughter of the Sun-god and who was represented with a child in her arms) was smoothly renamed as "Saint Bridget." In pagan days, her chief temple at Kildare was served by Vestal Virgins who tended the sacred fires. When the days of the falling away came, the temple became a *convent* and her vestals, *nuns!* They continued to tend the ritual fire dedicated to the Goddess, only it too was renamed and called "St. Bridget's Fire."[2]

The best preserved ancient temple now remaining in Rome is the PANTHEON which in olden times was dedicated (according to

1. Man and His Gods, p. 227; Durant, p. 745; Doane, p. 396.
2. Festivals, Holy Days, and Saints' Days, p. 26.

34

the inscription over the portico) to "Jove and all the gods." However, it was reconsecrated by Pope Boniface IV to "The Mother of God and all the saints." Another pagan temple at Rome which was formely sacred to the "Bona Dea" (the Good Goddess), was "Christianized" and dedicated to the Virgin Mary. In a place formely sacred to the god Apollo, there now stands the church of St. Apollinaris! And where there anciently stood the temple of Mars, may now be seen the church of St. Martine![1]

In a further attempt to merge paganism into Christianity, church leaders of the falling away taught that Jesus was born in a cave! Of course there is no scriptural authority for such an idea. To the contrary, the cave that is shown at Bethlehem as the birth place of Jesus is actually a rock shrine in which the Babylonian god TAMMUZ was worshipped! This was mentioned by Jerome, a noted Christian writer of the Fourth Century.[2]

And so, throughout the Roman Empire, paganism died only to live again in the Roman Catholic church! Pagan temples and shrines were renamed. The pagan gods and goddesses were also renamed and their worship continued—now posing as Christian saints! And in merging all of this paganism into Christianity, not only did the devotion to the old idol gods continue, but even as the pagans had idols or statues of their gods, so the Roman Catholic church also adopted the use of statues into their worship.

In some cases, the very same statue that had been worshipped as a pagan god was renamed as a Christian saint—and the devotion continued! A statue of Jupiter, for example, was slightly changed and renamed as "Peter" (which we will mention in a later chapter). Other idols and statues were "Christianized" and Satan's old pagan idolatry continued—now in disguise. And through the centuries, more and more statues have been made and venerated, until today there are churches in Europe that contain as many as two, three, and four THOUSAND statues.[3] Whether in great impressive Cathedrals, in small chapels, at wayside shrines, on the dashboards of automobiles, or smiling frozenly in the cluttered dens of harlots—in all these places the idols of Catholicism may be found in abundance. And the use of such idols and images clearly identifies the Roman Catholic church as a continuation of paganism, not the pure, undefiled, church spoken of in the Holy Scriptures. Matt 16x8

The use of idols—regardless of what name men may place upon them—is Babylonish; for, as Herodotus mentions, Babylon was the source from which ALL systems of idolatry flowed to the nations.

1. Bible Myths, p. 396.
2. Epistle Ad Paulinum.
3. Encyclopedia of Religion and Ethics, art. "Images and Idols."

35

Repeatedly God has warned his people not to follow the practice of using idols in their worship:

The Bible says: "Thou shalt not make unto thee ANY graven image, or any likeness of anything that is in heaven above, or that is in the earth beneath, or that is in the water..."(Ex. 20:4). "Ye shall make you no idols nor graven image..."(Lev. 26:1). "Idolaters... shall (not) inherit the kingdom of God"(1 Cor. 6:9, 10). "Little children, keep yourselves from idols"(1 John 5:21).

Quite plainly then, the scriptures are AGAINST the use of idols and images in church worship. The early church—the true church —never used them. But when the "falling away" came, and paganism and Christianity were mixed together, free and full use was made of the old pagan idols to which the "church" fell heir. Apostate church leaders felt that since some of these statues were so valuable—some covered with silver and gold—they should be re-dedicated and their use continued. But what does God say about such reasoning? "The graven images of their gods shall ye burn with fire", our Lord commanded, "thou shalt not desire the silver or gold that is on them, nor take it unto thee, lest thou be snared therein; for it is an abomination to the LORD thy God" (Deut. 7:25).

And not only were the Israelites to destroy the idols of the heathen nations they conquered, but they were to "destroy all their PICTURES" also (Numbers 33:52). These were pictures of heathen deities. And so, not only is the use of idols condemned in the scriptures, but since pictures are often venerated in a superstitious way, these too bring no virtue to true worship. It is strange that some religions will condemn the use of statues, yet will make full use of pictures of the statues! But what difference is there? The statue is three dimensional, while the painting is on a flat surface. But neither was used by the apostles or the church of the New testament. It was not until the FIFTH century that pictures of Mary, Christ, and the "saints", were made and used as objects of worship. And even as the pagans placed a *circle* or aureole around the heads of their gods, so the fallen church continued this practice in connection with her "saints." The illustration at the right is the way St. Augustine is shown in Catholic books—with a circular

Babylonish

disk around his head. All of the "saints" of Catholicism are pictured in this same way. But to see that this practice was borrowed from heathenism, we need only to notice the drawing of Buddha at the right which also features the circular symbol around his head! Actually, this practice is Babylonish, for the artists and sculptors of ancient Babylon used the disk or aureola around any being they wished to represent as a god or goddess.[1] This custom continued among pagan religions even until the days of the Roman

Empire. The illustration at the left shows the way the Romans depicted Circe, the pagan goddess daughter of the sun, with a circle surrounding her head. From its use in pagan Rome, the same symbolism passed into Papal Rome and has continued to this day, as evidenced in thousands of paintings and pictures of "Mary" and of the "saints."

When the falling away came, pictures that were suppose to be portraits of Christ were painted with "golden beams" surrounding his head. This was exactly the way the sun-god of the pagans had been represented for centuries! And so this was but another compromise in the attempt to merge paganism and Christianity together.

Today both Catholic and Protestant churches (for the most part) make use of pictures of Christ. But the scriptures do not give us any description of the physical features of Jesus. No picture was made of him during his earthly life. The church of the first four centuries had no pictures of him. It is evident then that the so-called pictures of Christ, like those of Mary and the saints, are only the product of artists' imaginations. We only have to make a short study of religious art to find that in different centuries and among different nationalities, many different pictures of Christ—some very different—may be found. Obviously all of these can not be what Jesus looked like, for they differ one from the other!

Let us suppose that someone that had never seen you, knew nothing of your features, and had no way to know what you looked like—suppose they decided to paint a picture of you! Of course the finished picture would look nothing like you. Suppose then

1. Ancient Pagan and Modern Christian Symbolism, p. 35.

they put your name under it and told people that this was a picture of you. Would you appreciate this? Of course not. And neither should we think that Christ has ever put his approval upon men's conceptions of what they *think* he looked like!

I know that to write these things is not popular. But I believe that we can all agree that no man—not even the best artist in the world—could ever portray our Lord in his true and full glory! Any picture, even at its best, is a poor substitute—a mere image or idol in modified form—and such can never show how wonderful our Lord *really* is. True worshippers must worship God "in Spirit and in truth" (John 4:24) and the veneration of pictures, images, or idols, does not help true worship, it hinders it.

CHAPTER FIVE

Obelisks, Temples, and Towers

MONG THE ANCIENT heathen nations, not only were statues
of the gods and goddesses in *human* form made, but many
objects were venerated that had a symbolical, a hidden, a
MYSTERY meaning! An outstanding example of this
can be seen in the worship of the ancient obelisks,
one of which is seen in the accompanying illustration.

Diodorus says that Queen Semiramis erected an
obelisk at Babylon which was 130 feet in height.[1]
And so we know that the obelisks were used in the
religion of Babylon. But it was especially in Egypt
that their use became the most prominent. (As is
well known, Egypt became a great stronghold for
paganism and the Mystery system from the earliest
times.) There are a number of these ancient obelisks
that are still in Egypt, though a number of them have
been removed to other nations. One is in Central
Park in New York, another in London, and many of
them (as we shall see) were transported to ROME !

Originally, these obelisks were associated with
sun-worship. They were symbols of Nimrod or
Baal in deified form.[2] Those ancient people—having
rejected the knowledge of the true creator—seeing
that the sun gave life to plants and to man, looked
upon the sun as God, the Great Life Giver. But not
only were the obelisks sun-symbols, they were recognized as sex-
symbols also. These ancient people knew that through the sex
act, life was produced. And so—as is well known by all who study
into it—the phallus (the male organ of reproduction), was also
considered (along with the sun) as a symbol of life—and as such,
a symbol of their sun-god. And it was this sun-sex belief that was
symbolized by the obelisk![3]

1. Encyclopedia of Religions, Vol. 3, p. 264.
2. Fausset, p. 511.
3. Encyclopedia of Religions, p. 33; Ancient Pagan and Modern Christian Symbolism, p. 99.

39

Sun and sex

Considering then the vile significance of the obelisks, we need not be surprised to find that their use was forbidden in the Bible. The word "images" that appears in our Bible is translated from several different original words, having different shades of meaning. One of these words is *"matzebah"*, meaning "standing images", that is, obelisks. This word is used in 1 Kings 14:23; 2 Kings 18: 4; 23:14; Jer. 43:13; Micah 5:13. Another original word that often refers to the obelisks is *"hammanim"*, which means "sun-images"; that is, images dedicated to the sun, or obelisks. This word is found in the original text of Isaiah 17:8 and 27:9.

Now in order for these obelisks to carry out their heathenistic symbolism, they were placed upright—*erect*. Thus they pointed UP—toward the sun. As a symbol of the phallus, the ERECT position also had an obvious significance. Considering how important this erect position of an obelisk was to those worshippers of the Mysteries, it is interesting to notice what God said in warning of his wrath against such false worship. Our Lord declared that their "images"—obelisks—"shall not stand up" (Is. 27:9). Thus our Lord's displeasure with these erect images, the obelisks, is plainly revealed!

When the backslidden children of Israel mixed heathen worship with their worship of the true God, they too erected an "image of jealousy in the *entry*" of the Temple! (Ez. 8:5). This image was probably an obelisk, the symbol of the phallus; for, as Scofield says in commenting on this chapter, these people were "given over to PHALLIC cults."[1] This practice of placing an erect obelisk at the entrance of a heathen temple was an established custom of the time. An obelisk stood at the entrance of the temple of Tum, for example, as well as in front of the temple of Hathor, the "abode of Horus" (Tammuz).[2]

Considering the use of the obelisk at the ENTRANCE of the temples of ancient paganism, we need not be too alarmed to find *exactly* the same thing in connection with modern Babylon—the Roman Catholic church! Yes, not only was an obelisk placed at the entry of the temples of the ancient sun-worshippers, but in front of the entrance of ST. PETER'S CATHEDRAL at Rome, the *very same* symbol is found today! The photo on the following page shows St. Peter's church—*posing* as the "Mother" church of all Christianity—and right before it stands the image of jealousy, the obelisk, a symbol of the phallus! Here then is an amazing clue to help us identify modern Babylon.

1. Scofield Bible, p. 847, note.
2. Encyclopedia of Religions, p. 33.

40

How is it that this very abominable thing came to be placed here? As we study into this, we discover that as the Mystery religion spread to Rome, along with it came the use of the obelisk as a symbol. And not only were obelisks made and erected at Rome, but the very obelisks of Egypt—at great expense—were hauled to Rome and erected by the emperors and dedicated to the sun-god in pagan days. And such was the case with the obelisk that stands before St. Peter's. It is not a mere *copy* of an Egyptian obelisk, but it is the *very same* obelisk that was worshipped in Egypt in ancient times! Caligula, in A.D. 37-41, had this obelisk transported from HELIOPOLIS, Egypt, to his circus on the Vatican Hill, where now stands St. Peter's Cathedral.[1] Now Heliopolis, the city from which the obelisk was originally transported, is but the Greek name of Bethshemesh, which was the center of Egyptian sun-worship in olden days! And this was the very place of which we read in the Bible of the false worship that existed there and in which special mention is made of the "images (obelisks) of Bethshemesh (the House of the Sun)"(Jer. 43:13)!

And so, the very same obelisk that once stood at the ancient pagan temple at the CENTER of Egyptian paganism (Heliopolis or Bethshemesh) now stands before the temple that is the CENTER of modern paganism—the so-called Cathedral of St. Peter, the "Mother" church of Catholicism. This seems like more than a mere coincidence.

The red granite obelisk of the Vatican is itself 83 feet high (132 feet high with its foundation) and weighs 320 tons. In 1586, to make certain that this obelisk was centered right directly at the entry of the Cathedral, it was moved a short distance to its present location—St. Peter's square—by order of Pope Sixtus V. Of course the moving of this heavy obelisk—especially in those days—was a very difficult tast. Many movers refused to attempt the feat, especially when the Pope had attached the DEATH PENALTY if the obelisk was dropped and broken.[2] (Such a regulation in itself indicates how much importance that the Pope and his people accredited to this abominable idol!)

Finally a man by the name of Domenico Fontana accepted the responsibility of the moving and erection of the Vatican obelisk. With 45 winches, 160 horses, and a crew of 800 workmen, the task of moving began! The date: September 10, 1586. Multitudes crowded the extensive square. While the obelisk was being moved, the crowd—UPON PENALTY OF DEATH—was required to remain silent until the erection was made. (Again we see how

1. Harper's Bible Dictionary, p. 500; Catholic Encyclopedia, Vol. 13, p. 371.
2. Ancient Monuments of Rome, p. 175-177.

42

much importance the Romish church attributed to this idol!)
Finally, after near failure, the obelisk was erected—to the sound
of hundreds of bells ringing, the roar of cannons, and the loud
cheers of the multitude. The idol was dedicated to the "cross",
mass was celebrated, and the Pope pronounced a blessing on the
workmen and their horses.[1]

The accompanying drawing
shows how the cross-shaped
St. Peter's Cathedral and circular court in front of it are
layed out. In the center of this
court (A) is the pagan obelisk.
This circular court is formed
by 248 Doric style columns
which cost approximately One

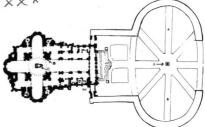

Million dollars! Now the use of such pillars was borrowed directly
from the styling of pagan temples! We show here below a drawing

of the old temple of Diana, as
one of many examples of how the
columns were used in heathen
temples. And, like the obelisk,
the columns were often regarded as "Mystery" forms of the
phallus. In the vestibule of the
pagan temple of the goddess at

Hierapolis, for example, an inscription referring to the columns
reads: "I, Dionysus, dedicated these *phalli* to Hera, my step-
mother."[2] And yet these columns were used in abundance to form
the circular St. Peter's square which surrounds the Egyptian
obelisk. Certainly such symbolism did not originate in Christianity!

Even the choosing of the Vatican Hill for the location of the
"Mother" church of Catholicism was the result of a mixture with
paganism. You see, in olden times, this hill, as the very word
indicates, was "a place of divinations" *(Vaticinia)*. The name is
said to have come from the name of the Divination-deity VATICANUS
who had headquarters on this hill![3]

Then at a later period, the hill was used for the annual festivals in honour of Attis or Tammuz, son of the Great Mother. At
this festival a pine tree was felled and to its trunk an effigy of the
god was fastened. This effigy was later buried in a tomb. Such
rites are still carried on today in all Catholic countries—rites

1. Ibid, p. 177.
2. Hastings, Art. "Phallism."
3. Ancient Monuments of Rome, p. 75.

that are a *mixture* of ancient paganism with Christianity. Since some of the ancient rites in honour of Tammuz were similar to events that had happened in the life of Christ (his death, burial, etc.), paganism and Christianity were merged "almost without interruption, for these pagan ceremonies were enacted in a sanctuary on the VATICAN HILL, which was afterward taken over by the (Roman Catholics) and the Mother church of St. Peter now stands upon the VERY SPOT"![1]

Even as Catholic leaders borrowed other things from paganism, we need not be surprised that they also copied the idea of building elaborate and expensive temples—as their main church, St. Peter's, which is the largest church in Christendom. The worldly minded church thought they should build such a *temple*—a temple of greater splendor than those of the old Roman religion. And so, fashioning its design after the pattern of the Pantheon of pagan Rome, only more elaborate, St. Peter's was finally completed at an estimated cost of 50 million dollars! And to this day, many still suppose that God wants his people to build costly and elaborate temples of worship. In fact, church construction has become big business!

But is the practice of putting multiplied thousands and sometimes millions of dollars into a fancy church building in accordance with the scriptures? Did Jesus or the Apostles give any such plan or teaching? What is God's plan in this connection?

We know that God directed his people under the rulership of King Solomon to build a temple—in the Old Testament—and the Lord chose to put his presence there. But coming to the New Testament, the Holy Spirit no longer dwells in temples made with men's hands (Acts 17:24). Now, God dwells in his *people*—his true church —by the Spirit! And so, says Paul: "YE are the temples of God... the Spirit of God dwelleth in YOU"(1 Cor. 3:16).

Understanding this truth, the early church—FILLED WITH THE SPIRIT—never went forth to build temples of stone and steel! They went forth to preach the gospel of the Kingdom—the message of that glorious kingdom to come. Emphasis was never put on a building. They did not resort to financial drives and oppressive pledges in an attempt to build a fancier building than a temple down the street! No, their time and money was put into the MESSAGE, not a building. In fact, we have no record of a church building (as such) being erected prior to 222-235 A.D.![2]

Of course we do not mean to suggest that it is wrong to have a church building. No doubt the reason why church buildings were

1. The Paganism in Our Christianity, p.123; A Traveler in Rome, p.270.
2. Halley's Bible Handbook.

not built earlier was because the first Christians were not allowed to own title to property, due to the persecutions which they
faced. But had they been allowed this privilege, we feel certain
that such buildings would have been built *simply*—not for outward
show. They would not have tried to compete with the expensive
styling of the heathen temples of splendor—like the temple of
Diana at Ephesus or the Pantheon of Rome.   Feb 11, 2010

But the fallen church of Rome—through compromise and mix- AD
ing with the world—came to political power and great wealth under
the reign of Constantine. They set a pattern for building expensive
church buildings—a pattern that has been followed to this day—a
pattern of building church edifices far more elaborate than what
is necessary. And this idea has become so implanted in the minds
of the people, that the word "church" (to most people) means a
BUILDING; whereas, the word church, in its true Biblical meaning, refers to a group of people who are—themselves—the temples of the Holy Spirit!   Steeple?

Now the majority of the expensive church buildings that have
been built through the centuries, have featured a TOWER. And so
we ask: Why do Roman Catholic churches almost invariably have
a tower? Why do most Protestant churches also follow this pattern
of featuring a tower in connection with their buildings of worship?
Each generation of church builders have copied the former generation, never questioning the origin of the idea.

Some church towers have cost fortunes to build. But for what?
Obviously they have not spiritual value. The millions of dollars
that have been spent on these towers could have gone toward the
furtherance of the gospel or to help those in need. It seems evident
that the only purpose for such towers is for mere outward show.
Of course there is no instruction in the Bible to build such towers.
Our Lord never built such a structure when he was here, nor did
he give any instructions like this to be followed by the disciples
after his departure. How then did this tower-tradition in church
architecture begin?

We are all familiar with the great tower of Babel and how God's
displeasure was displayed against it. We have seen how various
other ideas spread from Babylon. Could this be the source of the
idea of featuring a tower in connection with buildings of religion?
During those early days of Babylon, the people said: "Go to, let
us make brick... let us build us a city and a tower, whose top may
reach unto heaven"(Gen.11:3,4). Now the expression "unto heaven"
is no doubt a figure of speech for great height. Such an expression
is also found in Deuteronomy 1:28 which mentions cities whose

45

advertise location
bell towers

Watch Tower & Tract Society — religious Tower of Jehovah Witness).

walls reached "up to heaven." Likewise, the tower of Babel was to be a tower of great height. But we are not to suppose that the Babel builders intended to build clear up into the heaven of God's throne! No, they did not desire to be in His presence! Instead, there is sufficient evidence to show that the tower was connected with their religion—with sun-worship.

Historians refer to the Babel tower as a "Ziggurat." "Of all the lofty monuments of Babylon, the towering 'Ziggurat' must certainly have been one of the most spectacular constructions of its time, rising majestically above its huge encircling wall of a thousand towers... around the vast square, chambers were set aside for pilgrims, as well as for the priests who looked after the 'Ziggurat', and Koldewey called this collection of buildings the 'Vatican of Babylon'."[1] So while Babylon was famous for its huge tower of long ago, it also had numerous *other* towers for which it was known.

Goddess   It has been suggested that one of the meanings of the name of the Goddess Astarte (Semiramis), written as "Asht-tart", means "the woman that made towers."[2] The Goddess Cybele (who also has been identified with Semiramis) was known as the tower bearing goddess, the first (says Ovid) that erected towers in cities and thus was represented with a tower-like crown on her head, as was also Diana (See cut on page 17). In the symbolism of the Catholic church, a tower is emblematic of the virgin Mary![3] So we see a definite connection between the mother-goddess worship and the towers of Babylonian religion.

Now some of the ancient towers were built for military purposes —for watchtowers—as we all know. But many of the towers that were built throughout the Babylonian Empire were exclusively *religious* towers, associated with sun-worship, connected with a temple! In those times, a stranger entering a Babylonian city would have no difficulty in locating the temple, we are told, for high above the flat roofed houses, ITS TOWER COULD BE SEEN![4]

Each town in the Babylonian Empire had its temple and each temple had its tower.[5] We have seen how certain other basic ideas originated in Babylon and spread to the nations, and so it is not out of reason that Babylon was also the original source of the towers of religion! Especially does this seem probable when we remember that it was while they were building the huge tower of Babel that the dispersion began. As men migrated to the various lands, they took the idea of a "tower" with them. And though through the ages since that time, these religious towers have developed into different forms in different countries, yet the towers in one form or

1. Ancient Cities and Temples.
2. Two Babylons, p. 307.
3. A Dictionary of Symbols, p. 326.
4. The Cambridge Ancient History—Egypt and Babylonia, vol. 1, p. 533.
5. The Greatness that was Babylon, p. 355.

Islam Minarets

46

another remain! Let us briefly notice how towers are used by the different religions of the world:

Towers have long been an established part of the religion of the Chinese. The accompanying illustration shows one of their many "pagodas." (The root meaning of this word is "goddess"!) Concerning the towers used by the Hindu religion, we read: "Scattered above the large temple inclosures are great pagodas or towers...rising high above the surrounding country, everywhere they could be seen by the people, and thus their devotion to their idolatrous worship was increased... Many of these pagodas are several hundred feet high, and are covered with sculptures representing scenes in the lives of the gods of the temple, or of eminent saints."[1]

Among the Mohammedans also, though in a somewhat different form, can also be seen the towers of religion. The accompanying illustrations show (left) the numerous towers, called minarets, at Mecca. Towers of this style were also used at the famous Church

of St. Sophia at Constantinople (right).

And the use of towers is also carried out by Christendom—Catholic and Protestant. The tower of the great Cathedral of Cologne rises 515 feet above the street; while the Protestant cathedral of Ulm in Germany has one 528 feet in height. Not only on great Cathedrals, but even on small chapels, a tower of some kind is usually included in the design. And the only reason for so doing is simply because of tradition—a tradition that is never questioned.

At the top of many of these church towers, a spire often points to the sky! Actually, the spire or steeple—which is so familiar to us all and in such general use that its origin is seldom questioned—is just a modified form of the obelisk, of which we spoke in

1. The Story of the World's Worship, p. 269.

the first part of this chapter! Numerous writers mention how the spire or steeple was originally but another form of the obelisk—a symbol of the phallus.[1] "There are still in existence today remarkable specimens of original phallic symbols...steeples on the churches...and obelisks...all show the influence of our phallus-worshipping ancestors." (Customs of Mankind, p. 55.)

At the top of the spire or steeple on churches, a cross is almost invariably placed. The expensive Cathedrals and church buildings of which we have written in this chapter, are often decorated with crosses in many ways. At the top of the obelisk that stands at the entry of St. Peter's, a cross has been placed to "Christianize" it. But is the *cross*, as an image, a piece of wood, really a Christian symbol? It is this question that we discuss in the chapter that follows...

1. Isis Unveiled, p. 5; Ancient Pagan and Modern Christian Symbolism, p. 14.

CHAPTER SIX

Is the Cross a Christian Symbol?

THE CROSS IS recognized as one of the most important symbols of the Roman Catholic church. It is displayed at top of the roofs and towers of their churches. It is seen on their altars, furnishings, and ecclesiastical garments. The floor plan of the majority of Catholic churches is laid out in the shape of the cross. All Catholic homes, hospitals, and schools have the cross adorning the walls. Everywhere the cross is outwardly honoured and adored — in hundreds of ways!

In like manner, the *sign* of the cross is often used in the Catholic rites. When an infant is sprinkled, the priest makes the sign of the cross upon the infants forehead saying: "Receive the sign of the cross upon thy forehead." During confirmation, the candidate is signed with the cross. On Ash Wednesday, ashes are used to make a cross on the foreheads of Catholic members. When they enter the church building, they dip the forefinger of the right hand in "holy water", touch the forehead, the chest, the left and the right shoulder—thus tracing the figure of the cross. The same sign is made before eating meals. During Mass, the priest makes the sign of the cross 16 times and blesses the altar with the cross sign 30 times.

Protestant churches, for the most part, do not believe in making the sign of the cross with their fingers. Neither do they bow down to it or use it as an object of worship. They have recognized that these things are unscriptural and superstitious. But they have made use of the cross on their steeples, on their church roofs, on pulpits, and in various other ways. And so, to one degree or another, Christendom—both Papal and Protestant—has assumed that there is virtue in the cross image; that our church buildings should be decorated with it; that it is a Christian symbol. But we ask: Is the cross which took our saviour's life a thing to be *adored?* Should we parade the instrument of death before the world and be *proud* of it? Do the scriptures anywhere teach that we are to take the cross and place it upon our buildings or wear it around our necks?

Personally, I had never questioned the use of the cross on churches and their furnishings. Like others, I assumed that the cross was a Christian symbol. But a study of historical evidence plainly reveals that the cross symbol is of PAGAN origin! The early Christians did not consider the cross as a virtuous symbol, but rather as "the accursed tree", a device of death and "shame" (Heb. 12:2). They did not trust in an old rugged cross. Instead, their faith was in *what was accomplished* on the cross; and through this faith, they knew the full and complete forgiveness of sin!

It was in this sense that the apostles preached about the cross and gloried in it (1 Cor. 1:17, 18). Such references to the cross in the epistles *never* refer to a PIECE OF WOOD one might wear around their neck or carry in their hand. The message of the apostles was concerning the ONE that hung and died on the cross. When they spoke of the cross, they were speaking of the suffering of Calvary, the Supreme Sacrifice that was made there, and the eternal purpose of God that was accomplished. But never did those of the early church consider a piece of wood as a protector, a good luck charm, or as an object of worship. No, such use of the cross came much later.

It was not until Christianity began to be paganized that the cross came to be thought of as a Christian symbol. It was in 431 A.D. that crosses in churches and chambers were introduced, while the use of crosses on steeples did not come until about 586 A.D.[1] In the 6th Century, the crucifix image was introduced and its worship sanctioned by the church of Rome.[2] It was not until the second council at Ephesus that private homes were required to possess a cross.[3] Such use of the cross then was obviously not a doctrine of the early *true* church. It was not a part of *"the* faith that was *once* delivered to the saints." From where then did it come?

In the following pages, we will give historical PROOF that the cross was an object of worship centuries *before* the Christian Era. We will see that the cross sign is Babylonish and that its entrance into the professing church was but a further attempt to

1. Harper's Book of Facts. 3. The Cross in Tradition, History, and Art, p. 157.
2. Fausset, p. 145.

50

mix paganism with Christianity:

Centuries before the Christian era, the cross was honored as a religious symbol by the people of Babylon. It is seen on their oldest monuments.[1] Historians say that it was a symbol associated with TAMMUZ.[2] But what was the significance of the cross symbol in Babylon and how was it associated with the false "saviour" Tammuz?

The cross symbol—in its original form—came from the first letter of the name Tammuz, the "T". "The same sign of the cross that Rome now worships was used in the Babylonian Mysteries", says Hislop, "...that which is now called the Christian cross was originally no Christian emblem at all, but was the mystic Tau of Chaldeans and Egyptians—the true original form of the letter T— the initial of the name of Tammuz... and was used in every variety of way as the most sacred symbol... it was used as an amulet over the heart; it was marked on the official garments of the priests, as on the official garments of Rome today."[3]

From Babylon, this cross symbol spread to Egypt, where monuments preserved to this day give abundant evidence of its use

there. In ANY book on Egypt that shows the old monuments and walls of their ancient temples, one can see the kings and gods of antiquity holding crosses in their hands. The accompanying illus-

tration shows some of the gods of Egypt in *mystery* form—part human and part animal—each holding a cross!

The illustration that we give here below is taken from a build-

ing of Amenophis IV at Thebes, Egypt. At the right the king is praying. Notice the round sun circle with a mystery form of the sun-god beneath it. Says a noted historian in

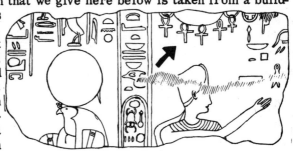

1. Doane, p. 342.
2. The Greatness that was Babylon, p. 496, 498.
3. Two Babylons, p. 197.

reference to Egypt: "Here unchanged for thousands of years, we find among her most sacred hieroglyphics the cross in various forms...but the one known specially as the 'cross of Egypt', or the Tau cross, is shaped like the letter T, often with a circle or ovoid above it, yet this mystical symbol was not peculiar to this country. but was reverenced...among the Chaldeans, Phoenicians, Mexicans, and EVERY ancient people in both hemispheres."[1]

As the cross worship spread to various nations, it took on varied forms and was used in varied ways: Among the Chinese, "the cross is...acknowledged to be one of the most ancient devices... it is portrayed upon the walls of their pagodas, it is painted upon the lanterns used to illuminate the most sacred recesses of their temples."[2]

The cross has been a sacred symbol in India for centuries among non-Christian people. "In Northern India, the cross is used to mark the jars of sacred water taken from the Indus and Ganges ...In Southern India the cross is used as an emblem of disembodied Jaina saints...The east Indians (revered the cross symbol)...centuries before our Lord appeared upon earth."[3] In the central part of India, two rude crosses of stone have been discovered which date back to a time centuries before the Christian era. One of these crosses is over 10 feet high; the other over eight feet.[4] Among the Hindoos of India, the cross was regarded as sacred to their god Agni.[5] The Buddhists, and numerous other sects of India, marked their followers on the head with the sign of the cross.

On the continent of Africa, "at Susa, in Abyssinia...the natives plunge a cross in the River Gitche...the Kabyle women although Mohammedans, tattoo a cross between their eyes...In Wanyam-wizi, or the land of the moon, the inhabitants decorate their walls with crosses...the Yaricks established a line of kingdoms from the Niger to the Nile...on their shields (was) painted the image of a cross."[6] Here then is mention of the use of the cross by numerous heathen tribes in Africa who knew nothing of Christ!

When the Spaniards first landed in Mexico, "they could not suppress their wonder", says Prescott, "as they beheld the cross, the sacred emblem of their own (Catholic) faith, raised as an object of worship in the temples of Anahuac. The Spaniards were not aware that the cross was the symbol of worship of the highest antiquity...(and was used by many) pagan nations on whom the light of Christianity had never shone."

In Palenque, Mexico, founded by Votan in the 9th century be-

1. The Cross in Tradition, History, and Art, p.2,3. 4. Ibid, p. 12.
2. Ibid, p. 13.   5. Monumental Christianity, p. 14.
3. Ibid, p. 10.   6. The Cross in Tradition, History p. 9.

52

fore the Christian era, is a heathen temple known as "the temple of the cross." There inscribed on an altar slab is a central cross six and a half by eleven feet in size![1] The illustration at the right shows this cross which was worshipped centuries before anyone in Mexico had ever heard of Christ!

In olden times, the Mexicans worshipped the cross as TOTA (Our Father). This practice of addressing a piece of wood with the title "father" is also mentioned in the Bible. When God's people of the Old Testament mixed idolatry with their religion, they worshipped pagan gods and said to a stock, "Thou art my Father"(Jer. 2:27)! But it is contrary to the word of God to call a piece of wood (or a priest!) by the title "father."

Ages ago in Italy, before the people knew anything of the arts of civilization, they believed in the cross as a religious symbol. Even at this early period, they believed it was a protector and it was placed upon tombs.[2] Through the centuries, it was used as a religious symbol right on up to the days of the pagan Roman empire. In 46 B. C., Roman coins show Jupiter holding a long scepter terminating in a cross.[3] This was his symbol.[4] The vestal Virgins of pagan Rome wore the cross suspended from their necklaces, as the nuns of the Roman Catholic church do now.[5]

The Greeks depicted crosses on the head band of their god corresponding to Tammuz of the Babylonians. (See illustration.) In the Eleusinian Mysteries, a cross was placed on the breast of each initiate.[6] Porcelli mentions how that Isis was shown with a cross on her forehead. Her priests carried processional crosses in their worship of her. The temple of Serapis in Alexandria was surmounted by a

cross. The temple of the Sphinx when it was unearthed was found to be cruciform in shape. Ensigns in the form of a cross were carried by the Persians during their battles with Alexander the Great (B. C. 335).[7]

The cross was used as a religious symbol by the Aborigines of South America in ancient times.[8] New born children were placed

1. Encyclopedia of Religions, vol. 3, p. 70.
2. The Cross in Tradition, History and Art, p. 22.
3. Ibid, p. 26.
4. Encyclopedia of Religions, Vol. 1, p. 495.
5. Two Babylons, p. 198.
6. Bible Myths, p. 343.
7. Ibid, p. 346.
8. Curiosities of Popular Customs, p. 297.

under its protection against evil spirits.   The Patagonians tattoed their foreheads with crosses.[1] Ancient pottery in Peru has been found that is marked with the cross as a religious symbol.[2]

Monuments show that Assyrian kings wore a cross suspended on their necklaces,[3] as did some of the foreigneers that battled against the Egyptians. These warriors wore a small cross suspended to a necklace or to their collar. The cross was also figured upon the robes of the Rot-n-no—as early as the 15th century before the Christian era.[4] (See cut.)

Much more could be said about the many uses of the cross as a religious symbol and object of worship among those who lived in olden times. But enough has been said to well establish the fact that the cross was in use long before the Christian era. To sum it up, there is hardly a pagan tribe where the cross has not been found.[5] "In some form, all through the ages, the cross has existed and has had a vital significance and influence."[6]

As an instrument of death, of crucifixion, the cross is also very ancient—and pagan. "The cross was used in ancient times as a punishment for flagrant crimes in Egypt, Assyria, Persia, Palestine, Carthage, Greece, and Rome... Tradition ascribes the invention of the punishment of the cross to a woman, the queen SEMIRAMIS"![7]

"But since Jesus died on a cross", some ask, "does this not make it a Christian symbol?" No. The fact that Jesus was killed on a cross shows that it was already an established form of punishment and death—among pagans. It was not a Christian symbol when Jesus hung on it, and nothing has ever changed to make it a Christian symbol now! As one has asked: Suppose Jesus had been killed with a shot gun; would this be any reason to have a shot gun hanging from our necks or on top of the church roof? Would this make a shot gun a Christian symbol of virtue? No. It is not *what* killed our Lord, but *what his death accomplished* that is important!

As the cross symbol spread to the ancient nations (as we have seen it did), it took on different forms in different countries until there were many forms of the pagan cross. Catholicism, adopting the pagan idea of cross worship, also adopted these various forms

1. Encyclopedia of Religions, Vol. 1, p. 495. 5. Two Babylons, p. 199.
2. Ibid, p. 386.   6. The Cross—Its History and Symbolism, p. 16.
3. Ibid, p. 494.   7. The Cross in Tradition, History, and Art, p. 64.
4. Wilkinson, Vol. 1, p. 376.

of the cross. Thus, to this day, the Catholic church does not adore just ONE type of cross, but numerous types, some of which are shown in the accompanying illustration. Now we ask: If the Catholic use of the cross originated with the cross of Christ, then WHY are so many *different* forms of the cross used? It is evident that Christ only hung on ONE cross.

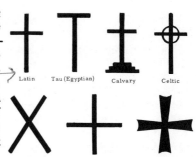

If cross worship originated with the cross of Christ, would it not seem that only *one* type would be used?

The fact is that cross worship did not originate with Christ and all of these various forms of the cross were pagan symbols before the Christian era. Says a noted writer: "Of the several varities of the cross still in vogue, as national and ecclesiastical emblems, distinguished by the familiar appelations of St. George, St. Andrew, the Maltese, the Greek, the Latin, etc., there is not one amongst them the existence of which may not be traced to the *remotest antiquity*"![1]

Let us notice a few examples of how these different crosses were actually sacred symbols long before the Christian era: That form of the cross which is known as the TAU cross was widely used in Egypt (as we have seen already). What is known as the GREEK cross may also be found on Egyptian monuments. This form of the cross was used in Phrygia where it adorned the tomb of Midas (B.C. 718).[2] In the ruins of Nineveh, a king is shown wearing a MALTESE cross on his bosom. The form of the cross that is today known as the LATIN cross was used by the Etruscans. Its use on an *ancient* pagan tomb with winged angels to each side of it, is shown in the accompanying illustration.

What has been called the ST. ANDREW'S cross was highly venerated among the Cumas in South America. It was regarded as a protector against evil spirits.[3] It appeared on the coins of Alexander Bala in Syria in 146 B.C. and on those of Baktrian kings about 140 to 120 B.C. (Needless to say, this was long before "St. Andrew" was ever born!)

1. The Pentateuch Examined, vol. 6, p. 113.
2. Doane, p. 344; The Cross in Tradition, p. 21.
3. Encyclopedia of Religions, Vol. 1, p. 494.

55

The cross which we show at the right is today called
the CALVARY cross, yet the cross in this illustration
is taken from an ancient inscription in Thessaly which
dates from a period prior to the Christian era!

Now the fact that these various forms of the cross
have ALL been adopted by the Romish Church, makes it
obvious that such cross-sacredness did not originate with the
cross of Christ, for he died on only ONE cross!

What type of cross was it upon which Jesus died? The word
"cross" in the Bible is translated from "stauros" which comes
from the root "sta", that is, "to stand." As far as the word itself
is concerned, there is no indication of any cross piece whatsoever.

In his scholarly "Expository Dictionary of New Testament
Words", W. E. Vine states that the Greek word "stauros" means
simply an upright stake and is "to be distinguished f r o m the
ecclesiastical form of a two beamed cross...(which) had its
origin in ancient Chaldea, and was used as the symbol of the god
Tammuz (being in the shape of the Mystic Tau, the initial of his
name) in that country and in ajacent lands, including Egypt...
In order to increase the prestige of the apostate ecclesiastical
system, pagans were received into the churches apart from re-
generation by faith, and were permitted largely to retain their
pagan signs and symbols. Hence the Tau or T, in its most frequent
form, with the cross-piece lowered, was adopted to stand for the
cross of Christ"(P. 256).

As to the exact shape of the cross upon which Christ hung,
we need not be too concerned, for it is not the shape of the cross
that is the important thing. It is the ONE that hung there and what
HE accomplished that is ALL important.

CHAPTER SEVEN

Constantine and the Cross

AN OUTSTANDING FACTOR that caused the adoration of the cross image to become firmly established in the church of the falling away was the famous "vision of the cross" and the "conversion" of the Roman emperor Constantine.

On the day before the Battle of Milvian Bridge, Constantine prayed to his sun-god and there appeared a cross—we are told—over the setting sun with the inscription: "In hoc signo Vinces"; that is, "In this sign conquer." The next day, Constantine advanced the battle behind a standard portraying a CROSS. He was victorious in this battle and professed conversion. Of course such a *seeming* victory for Christianity—the conversion of the emperor—as the result of the cross vision—did much to further the use of the cross in the Roman Church.

But are we to suppose that the LORD JESUS gave such a vision to the Emperor Constantine? Actually there is little reason to consider this vision as authentic, especially since it has no real historical basis. The only authority from whom the story has been gathered by historians is Eusebius, who confessedly was prone to edification and was accused as a "falsifier of history."

If Constantine ever did—in reality—have such a vision, we can be sure its author was *not* God. The very idea that our Lord would command a pagan emperor to make a military banner embodying the cross and to go forth conquering and killing in that sign, is altogether inconsistent with the general teaching of the Bible and with the spirit of true Christianity.

This Roman empire (of which Constantine was the head), had been described in the scriptures as a "Beast." Daniel saw four great beasts which represented four world empires. These were Babylon (lion), Medio-Persia (bear), Greece (leopard), and Rome.

Babylon   Medo-Persia   Greece   Rome

This fourth beast, the Roman Empire, was so horrible in the eyes of God that it could not be compared to any earthly beast. (Daniel 7:1-8). Considering then how wicked this beastly Roman Empire was in the eyes of God, are we to suppose that the *Lord Jesus* became the leader of this beast system? Or would Jesus give a wicked emperor a vision and tell him to kill and fight as his representative? Did Jesus ever tell his people to go forth to kill others under a cross-banner supposedly representing him? Of course not! The very basis of Christianity is opposed to the unfairness of war, hate, and murder. Why then should we suppose that Christ would tell Constantine to conquer in his name and sign to further the Beast system of Rome? Obviously, such a vision came not from our Lord Jesus Christ!

But if the vision was not of God, how was it that Constantine was converted as a result? The fact is that the "conversion" of Constantine was a hoax! Even though this man had much to do with the establishment of certain doctrines and customs within the fallen church, the facts plainly show that he was not truly converted—not in the Bible sense of the word. Historians admit that the conversion of Constantine was "nominal, even by contemporary standards."[1]

Probably the most obvious indication that he was not *truly* converted may be seen from the fact that AFTER his supposed conversion, he committed several *murders*—including the murder of his own wife and son! According to the scriptures, "no murderer hath eternal life abiding in him"(1 John 3:15).

Constantine's first marriage was to Minervina, by whom he had a son named Crispus. His second wife was named Fausta who bore him three daughters and three sons. Now Crispus, his first born son, became a great soldier and a help to his father in the battles. Yet, in 326—very shortly after directing the *Nicaean Council!*—Constantine had this son put to death. The story is that Crispus had made love to Fausta, Constantine's wife. At least he was so accused by Fausta. But this may have been her way of getting Crispus out of the way, so that *her* sons would have claim to the

1. Man and His Gods, p. 220.

58

throne! However, Helena, Constantine's mother, persuaded him that his wife "had yielded to his son." And so, Constantine had Fausta murdered also.[1]

But these were not the only murders he committed. About the same time that Constantine had his son murdered, he decreed the execution of Licinianus, his sister's son. Constantine also put Licinus, his sister's husband to death, even though he had promised her that he would spare his life![2]

After Constantine's supposed conversion, he still remained the Pontifix Maximus or High Priest of the pagan state religion.[3] As Pontiff, he was required to carry out the ceremonial of the traditional cult. Likewise, when he dedicated Constantinople, he used both pagan and Christian rites in the dedication. Further evidence of how Constantine attempted to unite and *mix* together both paganism and Christianity, is seen on coins of the period which he had made. On these coins he put a cross (to please the professing Christians) while on the same coins were representations of Mars or Apollo. While professing on one hand to be a Christian, yet on the other hand, he continued to believe in pagan magic formulas for the protection of crops and the healing of disease.[4]

Constantine did show numerous favours toward the Christian faith however. He abolished death by crucifixion. He gave interest and support to the Roman church and the "clergy." He stopped the persecutions of the Christians which had become so cruel at Rome. Why then, if he was not truly a Christian, did he do these things? The answer to this is also clearly written in history:

Persecutions had not destroyed the Christian faith. Constantine knew this. And since his position was being challenged by a rival emperor and because of his dire need for support from every quarter, he turned to the Christians. Instead of the empire constantly being *divided* —the pagans opposing the Christians—why not take such steps as might be necessary to MIX both paganism and Christianity together, and thus bring a UNITED force to the empire? This was clearly the reasoning of Constantine. By this time, most of the church leaders were thinking in terms of numbers and popularity, rather than in terms of spirituality and truth anyway, and thus were ready to make compromises with paganism. Especially was this the case at Rome.

So by adopting the cross as a symbol on the banners of his army, Constantine figured he could establish a UNITY among his troops. The apostate Christians would think they were fighting for the cross

1. The Story of Civilization—Caesar and Christ, p. 663. 3. The Growth of the Christian Church
2. Ibid, p. 663; Medieval Italy, p. 4.   4. The Story of Civilization, p. 656.

of Christ; the pagans could not object because the cross was also one of their sacred emblems. Says the noted historian Durant: "To the worshipper of Mithra (the pagans) in Constantine's forces, the cross could give no offense, for they had long fought under a standard bearing a mithraic cross of light."[1] And thus the so-called Christians and pagan Mithraists in the army of Constantine were united and successfully fought the battle.

Another factor that contributed to cross-worship in the church of Rome centered around *Helena*, Constantine's mother. In 326, when she was almost eighty—according to the legend—she made a pilgrimage to Jerusalem and there by the help of a Jew who understood her superstitious tastes, found three crosses. The original cross was identified—we are asked to believe—because it is said to have worked miracles at the suggestion of Macarius, bishop of Jerusalem. The other two crosses produced no miracles. And so Helena—according to the story—had found the original, the true cross! But that the true cross was found is no doubt false, for laws among the Jews required crosses to be burned after being used for crucifixion.[2]

That Helena did visit Jerusalem seems to be historically correct. But the story of her discovery of the original cross was evidently a later addition, for it did not appear until 440 A. D. — 114 years later! [3]

But let us just suppose that someone did find the actual cross upon which Jesus died. Would there be any virtue in that piece of wood? No, absolutely none. The Calvary cross served its purpose even as the brazen serpent had served its purpose when the children of Israel were bitten by snakes. We will remember that Moses had made a brazen serpent and raised it up on a pole. This was a type of the way that Christ was to be lifted up. (John 3:15). Nevertheless, after the brazen serpent had served its purpose, the Israelites kept it around and finally began to worship it. (2 Kings 18:4). They made it a relic and attempted to copy the heathenistic use of relics and mix it into their religion! And so Hezekiah "did that which was right in the sight of the Lord" by breaking the brazen serpent to pieces. In like manner, if we actually had the original cross—if it were still in existence—there would be no reason to set it up as an object of worship. Why? Because its purpose has been fulfilled. If then there would be no power in the ORIGINAL cross, how much less is there in a mere piece of wood in its shape? In view of these things, it becomes obvious that the use

1. Ibid, p. 655.
2. Fausset, p. 145.
3. Encyclopedia of Religions, Vol. 1, p. 494.

of the cross—in sign or symbol, in any shape or form—as an object of worship, is a mockery to true worship, which is the worship of Christ himself!

But each century brought more superstition into the Romish church in connection with the cross image. It came to be recognized as a protector. Had it not helped Constantine win the battle of Milvian Bridge? Had not the cross worked miracles for Helena? And so it came to be regarded as an image that could scare away evil spirits. It was worn as a charm. It was placed high up on church steeples to frighten away lightning. But because of the high position of the cross upon the steeple, it was often the very thing that caused lightning to strike the building! The use of the cross in private homes was supposed to ward off trouble and disease. And so even as the pagan Egyptians had set up obelisks, not only as a symbol of their god, but in some cases the very image was believed to possess supernatural powers, even so did people come to worship the cross. Thousands of pieces of wood —supposedly pieces of the "original cross"—were sold as protectors and charms. The account of this and how other relics rose to a place of popularity and worship is given in the next chapter...

CHAPTER EIGHT

The Relics of Romanism

THE GROSS SUPERSTITION that has accompanied the use of relics reveals the deception and inconsistency with which Romanism has been plagued for centuries. Some of these relics —as we shall see—are so obviously *false*, it seems hard to realize that people in this century of increased knowledge would still believe in them. Among the most common relics of the Catholic church have been the supposed pieces of the "true cross." But it is evident that all of these pieces could not have been a part of the original cross, for there were enough of them scattered through Europe to make a forest. The only explanation that could be given for this inconsistency was that the pieces had supernaturally multiplied even as the loaves and fish that were blessed by Christ!

Other relics that have received the approval of the various popes through the centuries include the following: nails from the cross, the sponge lifted to Christ's mouth, the purple coat which was thrown over his shoulders by the mocking soldiers, the crown of thorns, the cup at the last supper, specimens of the hair of the virgin Mary (some brown, some blond, some red, and some black!), skirts of the virgin, her wedding ring, her slippers, swaddling clothes of the baby Jesus, Joseph's carpenter tools, one of the thirty pieces of silver, the empty purse of Judas, Pilate's basin, and bones of the ass on which Jesus made his entry into Jerusalem!

The "Tabernacle of Mary Magdalene" claimed to have the towel Jesus used to wipe the disciples feet, the napkin that covered his face in the tomb, Mary's veil, some of her clothes, as well as a bottle of the virgin's milk![1] Some of Mary's milk is also supposed to have colored the walls of the place called the "Milk Grotto" at Bethlehem, and pieces of the chalk rock are sold as relic-charms!

Though we know nothing of the mother of Mary, not even her name—as Catholic scholars admit—yet a few hundred years ago, they gave to her the name of St. Anne. Soon many churches throughout Europe claimed to have her body as a sacred relic! One body was supposed to be in Apte, France, another in Lyons, and besides these bodies, she had a head at Treir, one at Turen, and still another at Turinge![2]

1. The Other Side of Rome, p. 53.
2. Ibid.

In about 750, long lines of wagons constantly came to Rome bringing immense quantities of skulls and skeletons. These were sorted, labeled, and sold by the Popes.[1] Such sales of dead bodies and bones became big business. Every *Romeo* (pilgrim to Rome) was anxious to acquire relics. Graves were plundered by night and tombs in churches were watched by armed men! "Rome", says Gregorovius, "was like a mouldering cemetary in which hyenas howled and fought as they dug greedily after corpses." There is in the church of St. Prassede a marble slab which states that in 817 Pope Paschal had the bodies of 2300 martyrs transferred from cemetaries to this church.[2]

The church at Coulombs, France, claimed to possess what was known as the "Holy Prepuce." (The prepuce is the tiny portion of skin that is removed from a baby boy when he is circumcised.) Just how the church in France came into possession of the supposed prepuce of Jesus so many years later is, of course, a mystery. Its powers were highly acclaimed, however. It was believed to have power to make childless women fertile and allow safety to women at childbirth. Even Henry V of England believed in its powers to the extent that when Queen Catherine was to have her child, an heir to the British throne, he made arrangements to borrow the prepuce. His wife had no complications in childbirth, and, consequently, out of appreciation for the help of the relic, he built a sanctuary at Coulombs for the safe keeping of the prepuce. The story spread. It was not long until churches in other areas claimed to possess the Holy Prepuce, including the church of St. John in Rome and the church of Puy in Velay![3]

Many of these "sacred relics" have been proven—beyond question—to be fakes. Some of the bones that were at one time acclaimed as the bones of saints and martyrs, for example, have been exposed as the bones of *animals!* In Spain, a Cathedral displayed what was said to be part of a wing of the angel Gabriel when he visited Mary. Upon investigation, however, it was found to be a magnificent OSTRICH feather![4]

In view of these many inconsistencies involved, why do Catholics ascribe so much importance to relics? One reason for this is that the placement of a relic in a chapel or cathedral is believed to "consecrate" the ground and building.[5] The Seventh Ecumenical Council of Nicaea in 787 forbade a bishop to dedicate a building if no relics were present; the penalty for so doing was excommunication from the church! So extreme did this belief become in the

1. Medieval Italy, p. 71.
2. Ibid, p. 391.
3. The Other Side of Rome, p. 54.
4. Roman Catholicism, p. 290.
5. Medieval Italy, p. 71.

middle ages, that some Cathedrals had THOUSANDS of relics. The Castle Church at Wittenberg, to the door of which Luther nailed his famous "95 Theses", for example, possessed 19,000 saintly relics! [1]

But where did the ideas about relics being necessary to "consecrate" the ground or buildings of a church originate? Certainly there is no indication of any such belief or practice by the Lord Jesus or the apostles! But, on the other hand, such use of relics was a definite part of PAGAN RELIGION!

When Nimrod, the false "saviour" of Babylon, died, his body was torn limb from limb, and his bones scattered over the country. This death is a striking *contrast* to the death of the true saviour, our Lord Jesus Christ. Nimrod was torn limb from limb, whereas, concerning Jesus it was prophesied: "A bone of him shall not be broken!" Bearing this in mind, let us go a little further:

When Nimrod was supposedly resurrected—becoming the sun-god—it was taught that he was now in a different body, the members of the old body being left behind. (Of course, such could not be termed a resurrection in the true sense of the word.) In the case of the Lord Jesus, however, he was *truly* resurrected. It was He, Himself, that rose again from the dead! The tomb was empty, no parts of his body were left behind for relics!

But in the legends of the death of the false "saviour", Nimrod, his body was torn to pieces—parts being buried here, and others there. As time went on, many places were believed to be a place where part of the body was buried and this ground was believed to be "consecrated", made sacred!

These ideas spread to other nations. Soon various places in Egypt, for example, were regarded as burial places of the martyred god. "Egypt was covered with sepulchres of its martyred god; and many a leg and arm and skull, all vouched to be genuine, were exhibited in the rival burying places for the adoration of the Egyptian faithful." [2]

Pilgrimages to such sacred burial places at an early period became a part of pagan religion. But true Christians need not make any pilgrimages to a tomb to worship some bones, for our saviour rose again and is alive forevermore! The tomb at Jerusalem is EMPTY! Yet in spite of this, so much paganism was absorbed into Catholicism, that during the middle ages, one of the most favorite ways of "washing away sin" was to make a pilgrimage to the Holy Sepulcher in Jerusalem!

1. Durant, Vol. 6, p. 339.
2. Two Babylons, p. 179.

64

Neither is there any basis in the scriptures for pilgrimages to the tombs of saints, martyrs, prophets, or apostles. In fact, the very way in which the Lord saw fit to dispose of the body of Moses, by burying it himself in the plains of Moab, so that no one knows his place of burial, would indicate our Lord's opposition to the idea of pilgrimages or the adoration of bones. (Deut. 34:6).

The influence of Egypt, the land from which the children of Israel had come, was evidenced in their sitting up of the golden calf. And since the land of Egypt was a place of multiplied relics, the wisdom of God in the secret burial of Moses is apparent. Years later, even the brass serpent that Moses made was named "Nehustan" and was worshipped as a sacred relic by the children of Israel (2 Kings 18:4). Now if they would practice such idolatry with something that Moses *made*, how much deeper in idolatry would they have gone if they had possessed one of his *bones!* And if it displeased God for those people to thus honour a relic then, certainly the use of relics displeases God now!

We have seen that many of the relics of Romanism are frauds —not the actual thing for which claims are made. But, let us suppose that we actually did have one of Mary's hairs, or a bone from the apostle Paul, or the robe that Jesus wore. Would the setting up of these things as sacred relics please God? According to the example of the brass serpent of Moses, they would not. And if there is no virtue in the *actual* hair, bone, or coat, how much less virtue is there in a *fake?*

It is not well known by many, but the word "chapel" comes from "capella"—the cape of St. Martin of Tours. The story is that St. Martin shared his cape with a beggar and later a vision was seen in which Christ himself was wearing it. The cape thus became a relic and was believed to possess great powers! It was carried into battle as a charm and was used as a surety for the verification of oaths. The Merovingian Kings kept it in the palace oratory where oaths were administered. Finally this room itself came to be known as the "capella" because of the cape that was kept there—the Capella S. Martini, the chapel of St. Martin, or simply, the chapel! The priest in charge of the royal oratory came to be called the "chaplain", for he was the "capellanus", the guardian of the cape. (See Webster's Dictionary; Catholic Encyclopedia, Vol. 3, p. 452; etc.).

CHAPTER NINE
Religious Fraud

THE SALE OF relics as well as pilgrimages to sacred shrines became *big business* for the fallen church of the middle ages. Pope Boniface VIII declared a jubilee for the year of 1300 and offered liberal indulgences to those who would make a pilgrimage to St. Peter's church that year. An estimated 2,000,000 people came. They deposited such treasure before the supposed tomb of St. Peter, that two priests, with rakes in their hands, were kept busy day and night raking up the money.[1] But what did the Pope do with this wealth? Much of it was spent to enrich his own relatives — the Gaetani — who with the money bought numerous Castles and splendid estates in Latium. Such action resulted in great resentment by the people of Rome.[2]

From the days of the supposed conversion of Constantine, the Roman church had continually increased in wealth—at a rapid pace. By the middle ages, the "church" owned entire cities, large portions of land, and possessed great riches. One of the ways that such wealth was obtained was through properties and money being *willed* to the church. In those days, very few people knew how to write. Consequently, a *priest* was usually called in to draft the wills. Of course with a priest drawing up the will, we can be sure that the Romish church was well remembered! And to make certain that a priest would draw up the will or that at least it would be drawn up under his supervision, Pope Alexander III decreed in 1170 that no one could make a valid will except in the presence of a *priest!* Any secular notary who drew up a will (except under these conditions) was to be excommunicated![3] Then too, often the last person to be with the dying man was the priest. For, according to Catholic dogma, the priest must give the last rites, the so-called Extreme Unction. At a time like this, if not before, large sums of money would be given to the priests, for masses, etc.

You see, in those middle ages (rightly called the *dark* ages), everyone in Catholic countries was required to belong to the Catholic church. There was nothing voluntary about it. If they were

1. The Story of Civilization, Vol. 4, p. 753; Medieval Italy, p. 485.
2. Ibid, p. 487.
3. The Story of Civilization, vol. 4, p. 766.

born in a Catholic country, they were automatically Catholics, even as we are automatically a citizen of the country in which we are born. And even as today each country requires that we pay a tax, so in that time the "Church" also charged a tax. Such money that was paid to the church was not the giving of free will offerings from the heart, but such fees were paid "of necessity" —a principle to which the Bible is opposed (2 Cor. 9:7). At every turn, the Catholic layman was required to *pay*—and this greatly enriched the fallen church.

Through the centuries additional money for the Catholic system has been derived from their system of *nuns*. Thousands of nuns work year in and year out to further the program of the fallen church. These—like the "vestial virgins" of ancient Rome —are not allowed to marry. Often they live a life of poverty and enjoy little freedom. Yet money flows continually to the bishops, cardinals, and the Pope who lives in an elaborate palace, reigns from a golden throne, wears regal robes and jewelled crowns!

Another money-maker of the Roman Catholic church was the selling of indulgences—pardons for sin! The idea that a person can *buy* with money a pardon for sin—past, present, or future— is not only unscriptural, but is absolutely contrary to the word of God. Such a practice is nothing short of BLASPHEMY against the precious blood of Christ, without which we cannot be cleansed from sin.

One of the many inconsistencies with such selling of indulgences was that those who sold them did not live a life that was any better than the sinners to whom they sold. About 1450, Thomas Gascoigne, Chancellor of Oxford University, complained of the Indulgence sellers of that day and the abuses that accompanied the practice. He said that the indulgence sellers would wander over the land and issue a letter of pardon, sometimes for the payment of two pence, sometimes for a glass of beer, for the hire of a harlot, or for carnal love.[1]

It was the selling of indulgences and its accompanying abuses that caused Martin Luther to begin what is known today as the Protestant Reformation. It is a very interesting story how it all came about: In order to raise funds for the construction work on St. Peter's church at Rome, a special drive was made by the Pope to sell indulgences. He employed several "high pressure" sales-men to do the selling and these men were sent to the various countries to make sales.

1. Ibid, Vol. 6, p. 23.

The man that was appointed to sell indulgences in Germany was John Tetzel. He had been convicted of Adultery and shameful conduct at Insbruck where his vices had almost cost him his life. The Emperor Maxmilian had ordered his death, but the Elector Frederick somehow secured his pardon.[1] He was known to be a man of poor conduct, but he did have ability as a quack fund raiser and thus was hired by the pope.

The following is an eyewitness description of Tetzel's entry into a certain German city: "When the... indulgence-seller approached the town, the Bull (the Pope's official document) was carried before him on a cloth of velvet and gold, and all the priests and monks, the town council, the schoolmasters and their scholars, and all the men and women went out to meet him with banners and candles and songs, forming a great procession; then with all the bells ringing and all the organs playing, they accompanied him to the principal church; a red cross was set up in the midst of the church and the Pope's banner was displayed; in short, one might think they were receiving God himself. In front of the cross was placed a large iron chest to receive the money, and then the people were induced in various ways, by sermons, hymns, processions, and bulletins, to buy indulgences."[2]

Tetzel preached that the indulgences were the most precious gift of God. So *extreme* did he become in his effort to make sales, he declared that by virtue of his certificates of pardon all the sins which the purchaser should afterward desire to commit would be forgiven him, and that "not even repentance is necessary"![3]

It is said that he carried with him a picture of the devil tormenting the souls of men in purgatory. He would frequently repeat the words that appeared on the money box he carried:

"Sobald der Pfenning im Kasten Klingt, Die seel' aus dem Fegfeuer springt." These words freely translated are as follows:

"Soon as the groschen in the casket rings, the troubled soul from purgatory springs."

Or, another translation: "As the money in you pop, the souls from purgatory hop."

And thus the rich gave large donations, while the poor poverty stricken peasant would sell all that he had to help his loved ones get out of "purgatory" or to pay for his own sins.

Now in those days, in Medieval universities, those who wished to advocate certain opinions would post up publicly "theses", that is, statements of their ideas, and invite all comers to discuss them. Following this custom, Martin Luther nailed his famous

1. History of the Reformation, p. 70.
2. Heresies of Rome, p. 84.
3. History of the Reformation, p. 71.

68

"95 Theses" to the door of the castle church in Wittenburg, Germany. These were 95 statements against indulgence selling (as the 27th against Tetzel's statement that as soon as the money goes in the collection box, the soul would hop out of purgatory) and similar abuses that were being made by the Pope and the Roman church.

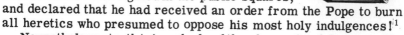

So Luther, though still a priest of Romanism, opposed the selling of indulgences. When Tetzel heard this, his face became red with rage. He uttered the most terrible curses in the pulpit, caused fires to be lighted in the public squares, and declared that he had received an order from the Pope to burn all heretics who presumed to oppose his most holy indulgences![1]

Nevertheless, truth triumphed and the abuse of indulgence selling and other errors of Romanism were exposed. Though the doctrine of indulgences is still believed by the Catholic church, the *selling* of indulgences and its accompanying abuses had to be subdued!

Financial abuse in other ways, however, has continued in the church of the falling away. Perhaps the greatest example of this may be seen in those fees that have been paid to have a priest "pray a loved one out of purgatory." The very idea that we could assure the salvation of one of our loved ones by the payment of money is utterly heathenistic—as we shall see. But adding to the contradition of such a position, there is no proof that any such purgatory exists; and even the priests must admit that they have no way of knowing when a person finally passes from purgatory into heaven! Such doctrines then are cruel and wicked! Is if any wonder that people will almost give all they have to priests when they have been taught since childhood that these priests can pray their loved ones out of the burning flames!

Actually, when all the facts are seen as they really are, this priestly game is far worse than any system of gambling, worse than fraud, and more brazen than the methods employed by criminals who get money under false pretences. To play upon the love and tender memories of bereaved people and to cheat them out of their oft-times hard-earned and scanty wages, is certainly a horrible thing to be done in the name of religion. Yet, through such methods, much of the wealth of the Catholic church has been gained.

But in no uncertain terms, our saviour condemned such practices. He spoke of priests who would "devour widows' houses, and

1. Ibid, p. 78.

69

for a pretence make long prayer"(Matt. 23:14). Yet, the Catholic priest will go to a widow—who having just lost her husband, being deeply grieved over the loss—and in this condition he will tell her that her husband is in purgatory; that she should pay him money so he will pray him out of purgatory and on into heaven. At a time like this, and under the pressure of the moment, large sums of money have been given to the Catholic Church.

High mass may cost as much as $1,000 dollars (or more) depending on the flowers, candles, and number of priests taking part. It is sung in a LOUD tone of voice. The low mass, on the other hand, is much less expensive—only six candles are used and it is repeated in a LOW voice. The Irish have a saying: HIGH money, HIGH mass; LOW money, LOW mass; no money, NO MASS!

If relatives have no money or refuse to pay for masses, their dead are called the "forgotten souls in purgatory." However, on November 2, "all Soul's Day", each year prayers are said for these forgotten souls. On this day a fervent appeal is made to the members of the Roman Catholic church to contribute money for the priestly prayers and the solemn Requiem Mass which is said on this day for the suffering souls forgotten by their relatives.

But is there some way that a Catholic can be sure someone will pay for masses for him after his death? Yes, he may assure this by joining the Purgatorian Society established in 1856. To this fund he must make a contribution at least once a year and then he is assured that, upon his death, there will be prayers said for him.

During the Second World War, the Archbishop of Winnipeg, Canada, in a letter dated March 1, 1944, urged all the Roman Catholic mothers to GUARANTEE the salvation of their sons from purgatory by the payment to him of $40 dollars for prayers and masses to be celebrated on their behalf.

But according to the scriptures, it is impossible for us to redeem a man's soul by giving money on his behalf. No matter how much money might be given, it can *never* redeem anyone! The Bible plainly says that we are "NOT redeemed with corruptible things as silver and gold...but with the precious blood of Christ, as a lamb without blemish and without spot"(1 Peter 1:18, 19). My friends, it is only as a person comes to Christ and receives the cleansing of that precious blood that he can be redeemed! To teach that *money* can redeem anyone is a mockery to the blood of Christ —which alone cleanseth from sin. (1 John 1:7).

The Bible says it is *hard* for a RICH man to enter into the kingdom of heaven (Matt. 19:23, 24). Yet, according to Catholic dogma, if a man has enough money to pay for the saying of masses in his behalf, he will be escorted to heaven. And so, in this case, the teachings of Romanism are the exact *opposite* of what the Lord Jesus taught. Think about it!

The Bible says: "They that trust in their wealth, and boast themselves in the multitude of riches; none of them can by any means redeem his brother, nor give to God a ransom for him." (Psalms 49:6, 7). Now if money cannot redeem our own brother that is alive, how could money redeem him if he is dead? If such a procedure will not work for our own brother, then how could it be done by a priest that is no relation?

Whether he be Pagan, Papal, Protestant, or Pentecostal—no priest or preacher can guarentee the salvation of anyone, living or dead, by any amount of money that may be given him for his prayers. God is not bribed with money; he hates a bribe. Woe be to any preacher that gives the impression that a person can send him money and then he can pray and all of the person's loved ones will be saved or blessed in some special way as a result. No man can do this and be honest—for money can never buy the blessings or gifts of God.

Peter knew this, and when the Samaria Sorcerer thought he could "buy" the gift of God with money, Peter rebuked him. "To hell with you and your money!" he said, "How dare you think you could buy the gift of God?"(Acts 8:20, Phillip's Version [1]). The Bible makes it very plain that money cannot buy the salvation or gifts of God! Certainly then, the payment of money for prayers could never free anyone from purgatory—even if such a place did exist!

The early Christians of the New Testament never believed in such a place as purgatory. The word appears no where in the Bible. The idea of purgatory and prayers for the souls in purgatory was not known in the professing church to any degree until 600 A.D. when Pope Gregory the Great made claims about a *third* state—a place for the purification of the souls before their entrance into heaven. It was not accepted as a dogma of the Catholic church, however, until 1459 at the Council of Florence. Ninety years later, the Council of Trent confirmed this dogma by cursing those who wouldn't accept the doctrine.[2]

1. We have given here this translation for its plainess of speech. To this, J. B. Phillips in a footnote adds: "These (words) are exactly what the Greek means. It is a pity that their real meaning is obscured by modern slang."
2. Heresies of Rome, p. 82.

During the Twelfth Century, a legend was spread which helped advance the idea of purgatory. It was claimed that St. Patrick had found the actual entrance to the place! According to the legend, St. Patrick, in order to convince some doubters, had a very deep pit dug in Ireland, into which several monks descended. When they returned, said the tale, they described purgatory and hell with discouraging vividness. In 1153, the Irish knight Owen claimed he had also gone down through the pit into the underworld and the account of his nether experiences had a tremendous success. Tourists came from afar to visit the pit. However, the financial abuses that developed became so bad that Pope Alexander VI ordered it closed as a fraud in 1497.[1] Three years later, however, Pope Benedict XIV preached and published at Rome, a sermon *in favor* of Patrick's purgatory![2]

Many ridiculous tales about the hereafter were advanced during those middle ages. Such were used to instill fear in the uneducated masses and many of these ideas, such as the doctrine of purgatory, have continued from generation to generation since. But the true *origin* of the idea of purgatory was in paganism *long before* the Christian era! Turning the pages of history far into the past, we find that such ideas were a part of pagan religions and philosophies. Plato, for example, who lived from 427 to 347 B. C., spoke of the Orphic teachers of his day "who flock to the rich man's doors, and try to persuade him that they have a power at their command, which they procure from heaven, and which enables them by sacrifices and incantation..to make amends for any crime committed by the individual himself, or his ancestors... Their mysteries deliver us from the torments of the other world, while the neglect of them is punished by an awful doom."[3] Here then is a clear description of purgatory three centuries *before* our Lord Jesus was born!

There is an *elaborate* description of purgatorial suffering in the sacred writings of Buddhism. There have been times when *so many* of the Chinese Buddhists would come to buy prayers for the deliverance of their loved ones in purgatory, that special shops for this purpose were set up. (See the illustration at the right.)

In the religion of Zoroaster,

1. The Story of Civilization, p. 735.
2. Encyclopedia of Religions, Vol. 2, p. 159.
3. Man and His Gods, p. 127.

72

souls are taken through twelve stages before they are sufficiently purified to enter heaven; and the Stoics conceived of a middle place of enlightenment which they called Empurosis, that is, a place of fire.[1] The Moslems also teach a doctrine of purgatory. Their teaching is that the angels Munnker and Nekir question them as to their religion and prophet when they die. Many of these then go into purgatory, according to their belief. However, if the Moslem priest is paid *enough* money, the soul finds deliverance!

And that this idea of giving money on behalf of the dead is of very *ancient* origin, is seen right in the Bible itself. In olden times, God warned his people not to mix heathenistic ideas with their worship. Among other things that were forbidden, they were not to give money "for the dead"(Deut. 26:14). The indication is that the idea of benefiting the dead by paying money was already in existence even at that early period! —and God warned against it.

So the idea of a purgatory, in one form or another, is very ancient and, as the writer of the **TWO BABYLONS** sums it up: "In every system, therefore, *except that, of the Bible*, the doctrine of purgatory after death, and prayers for the dead, has always been found to occupy a place."[2] But from what source did these various religions get their idea of a purgatory?

It is very possible that the belief in purgatory was but a later developement of ideas that were associated with the Molech worship of ancient times. It seems that the various pagan nations had the idea that fire was necessary to cleanse from sin. Since fire was believed to be the earthly representative of the sun-god, such ideas about fire were closely connected with ancient sun-worship. It was this false belief in the cleansing powers of fire that was behind the abominable rites of passing through the fire to Molech. Concerning this rite, God commanded his people: "Thou shalt not let any of thy seed pass through the fire to Molech" (Lev. 18:21; Jer. 32:35; 2 Kings 23:10). But neither passing through the fires of Molech worship, or passing through the fires of purgatory, can ever cleanse man from sin. It takes the blood of our Lord Jesus Christ to do that!

Molech was but another name for Bel or Nimrod.[3] And so the Molech rites were definitely Babylonish. Molech was known as the fire-god, and one of the meanings of the name Tammuz (supposedly Nimrod reborn) is: perfect (Tam) by burning (Muz)! Now we are beginning to see the *real* significance and origin of the basic ideas of purification by fire. These same pagan con-

1. Encyclopedia Britannica, Vol. 22, p. 660, 11th Ed.
2. P. 167.   3 Fausset

cepts later developed into the idea of purgatory *after* death. This idea spread to the nations and finally, along with other pagan ideas, was absorbed into the Roman Catholic church!

The rites in connection with this false god Molech were very cruel and wicked. He was worship-  ed "with human sacrifices...with mutilation, vows of celibacy and virginity, and devotion of the first born."[1] Sometimes he was represented as a horrible idol with fire burning inside in such a way as to burn and consume what was placed in his arms. In the accompanying illustration, the pagan priest has taken a baby from its mother to be offered to Molech. Lest the parent should relent in offering the child, a loud noise was made on drums to hide the screams. (The word for drums is *"tophim"* from which comes the word Tophet which is mentioned several times in the Bible as the valley where such sacrifices were made.) While the drums sounded, bands played, and priests chanted, human sacrifices were devoured in the flames.

How pitiful it is that men think they must pay for their sins with money or such cruel rites. But how wonderful is the good news of the Bible which tells us that the price has already been paid— paid by our Lord himself! Salvation is by grace—by favour we could never merit by money, human rites, or sacrifices. "For by grace are ye saved through faith; and that not of yourselves: it is the gift of God: Not of works, lest any man should boast." (Ephesians 2:8, 9).

1. Fausset, p. 481.

CHAPTER TEN

Was Peter the First Pope?

STANDING AT THE head of the Roman Catholic church is the Pope of Rome. This man—according to Catholic doctrine—is the head of the church and successor of the apostle Peter. According to this belief, Christ appointed Peter as the first pope, who in turn went to Rome and served in this capacity for twenty five years. Beginning with Peter, the Catholic church claims a succession of popes to this day and upon this belief, the ENTIRE framework of Catholicism is built. BUT do the scriptures teach that Christ ordained ONE man to be above all others in his church? Can we find any scriptural authority for the office of a pope, a supreme Pontiff? Did the early Christians recognize Peter as such? The answer to these questions is no! The scriptures plainly show that there was to be an EQUALITY among the members of Christ's church and that HE "is the HEAD of the church"(Eph. 5:23), *not the Pope!*

James and John, along with their mother, came to the Lord one time asking that one of them might sit on his right hand and the other on his left in the Kingdom. (In Eastern kingdoms, the two principal ministers of state, ranking next in authority to the monarch, were styled the vizier of the right and the vizier of the left.) Now if the Roman Catholic claim was true, Jesus would have answered that he had given the right hand place to Peter and that he did not intend to create any left-hand place! But to the contrary, here was the answer that Jesus gave: "Ye know that the princes of the Gentiles exercise dominion over them, and they that are great exercise dominion upon them, but it shall *not* be so among you"(Matt. 20:20-26; Mk. 10:35-43).

In other words, Jesus told his disciples that they were not to act like kings; they were not to wear crowns, they were not to set on thrones, they were not to pattern themselves after heathen rulers! Yet every one of these things have the popes done through the centuries! In this statement, our Lord plainly said that none of them was to set himself up as a ruler over the others. Instead, he taught an equality—clearly denying the principles that are envolved in having a Pope ruling over the church as the "bishop of bishops"!

That there was to be EQUALITY among the apostles is also seen in Matthew 23:4-10. In this passage, Jesus warned the disciples against using flattering titles such as "father"(the word "Pope" means Father), Rabbi, or Master. "For one is your master, even Christ", he said, "and all ye are brethern." Certainly then, the idea that one of them was to be exalted to the position of a Pope is at utter variance with the text.

But Roman Catholics are taught that Peter was so greatly superior to the other disciples that the entire church was built upon him! The verse that is used to support this claim is Matthew 16:18: "And I say unto thee, that thou art Peter, and upon this rock I will build my church; and the gates of hell shall not prevail against it."

However, if we take this verse in its setting, we can plainly see that the church was not built on Peter, but on CHRIST. In the verses just before, Jesus asked his disciples who men were saying that he was. Some said he was John the Baptist, some Elijah; others thought he was Jeremiah or one of the prophets. Then Jesus said, "But whom say ye that I am?" And Peter answered, "Thou art the Christ, the Son of the living God." Then it was that Jesus said, "Thou art Peter (petros—a stone, a rock), and upon this rock (petra—a mass of rock—the great foundation rock of truth that Peter had just expressed) I will build my church." The rock upon which the true church was to be built was connected with Peter's statement—"Thou art the Christ"—and so the true foundation upon which the church was built was Christ himself, not Peter.

Other verses also make it clear who the true foundation rock was. We know for certain that it was not Peter, for Peter himself declared that Christ was the foundation Rock (1 Peter 2:4-8). He also spoke of that Rock (Christ) as "the stone which was set at naught of you builders... neither is there salvation in any other..." (Acts 4:11, 12). The church was built on Christ, He is the true foundation, and there is no other foundation: "For other foundation can no man lay than that is laid, which is Jesus Christ" (1 Cor. 3:11).

It is obvious that the other disciples did not take our Lord's words—"Upon this rock I will build my church"—to mean that he was exalting Peter to be their pope, for two chapters later they asked Jesus a question about who was the GREATEST? (Mt. 18:1). Now if two chapters before, Jesus had stated that Peter was the one upon whom the church was to be built, if this verse proved that Peter was to be the Pope, then the disciples would have automatically known who was the greatest among them!

It was not until the time of Calixtus, who was bishop of Rome from 218-223, that Matthew 16:18 was first used in an attempt to prove that the church was built on Peter and that the bishop of Rome was his successor.

Let us now take a closer look at Peter—let us *compare* him with the Popes—and it will become apparent that Peter was not a Pope at all!

1. Peter was married. The fact that Peter was a *married* man does not harmonize with the Catholic position that a Pope is to be unmarried. The scriptures tell us that PETER'S WIFE'S MOTHER was healed of a fever. (Mk. 1:30; Mt. 8:14). Of course there couldn't be a "Peter's wife's mother" if Peter didn't have a wife!

However, some try to explain this discrepency by saying that Peter ceased to live with his wife. If so, did his wife leave him? Why? Was it incompatibility? Or maybe he left her? If so, he was a wife-deserter. In either case, he was a poor foundation upon which to build a church!

But the Bible plainly shows that Peter did NOT leave his wife! Twenty five years after Jesus went back to heaven, the Apostle Paul mentioned that the various apostles had wives—including Cephas. (1 Cor. 9:5). (Cephas was Peter's Aramaic name—John 1:42). Obviously Peter had not left his wife.

2. Peter would not allow men to *bow down* to him. When Peter was coming into the house of Cornelius, we read that "Cornelius met him, and fell down at his feet, and worshipped him. But Peter took him up, saying, Stand up; I myself am a man"(Acts 10:25, 26). This was quite different from what a pope would have said! Men bow to the pope and he loves to have it so.

3. The popes place *tradition* in a place equal to the Word of God. But Peter—to the contrary—had little faith in "traditions from your fathers"(1 Peter 1:18). Peter's sermon on the day of Pentecost was filled with the Word of God, not traditions of men. And when the people asked what they should do to get right with God, Peter did not tell them to have a little water poured or sprinkled on them. Instead, he said: "Repent and be *baptized* everyone of you in the name of Jesus Christ for the remission of sins, and ye shall receive the gift of the Holy Ghost"(Acts 2:38).

4. Peter was not the pope, for he wore no *crown*. Peter himself explained that God's people were not to wear crowns in this life, but that when the chief shepherd shall appear, THEN shall we "receive a crown of glory that fadeth not away"(1 Peter 5:4). Since Jesus has not yet appeared again, the crown that the Pope wears is surely not one that is bestowed upon him by Christ!

77

In short, Peter never acted like a Pope, Peter never dressed like a pope, Peter never spoke like a pope, Peter never wrote like a pope, and people did not approach him as a pope. Why? Because Peter was not a Pope!

In all probability, in the very early days of the church, Peter *did* take the most prominent position among the apostles. This we do not deny. It was Peter who preached the first sermon after the Holy Spirit came at Pentecost and 3,000 were added to the Lord the same day. Later, it was Peter who first took the gospel to the Gentiles. Whenever we find a list of the twelve apostles in the Bible, Peter's name is always mentioned FIRST (See Matt. 10:2; Mk. 3:16; Luke 6:14; Acts 1:13). But none of this — not by any stretch of the imagination — would indicate that Peter was the Pope or Universal Bishop of bishops!

While Peter apparently did take the most outstanding role of the apostles at the very beginning, yet later, PAUL seems to have had the most outstanding ministry. As a writer of the New Testament, for example, Paul wrote 100 chapters with 2,325 verses, while Peter only wrote 8 chapters with 166 verses. Thus Paul's ministry became more far reaching than that of Peter.

In Galatians 2:9, Paul spoke of Peter, James, and John as pillars in the Christian church. Yet Paul could say, "In NOTHING am I behind the very chiefest apostles"(2 Cor. 12:11; 11:5). But if Peter had been the SUPREME pontiff, the Pope, then certainly Paul would have been somewhat behind him! Obviously this was not the case. Then in Galatians 2:11, we read that Paul gave a rebuke to Peter "because he was to be *blamed.*" From this it seems evident that Peter was not regarded as an "infallible" Pope!

It was Paul that was "THE apostle of the Gentiles"(Romans 11: 13), whereas Peter's ministry was "unto the circumcision"(Gal. 2: 7-9). This fact—in itself—would seem like sufficient proof that Peter was not Bishop of ROME, as Catholics are taught, for Rome was a Gentile city. All of this is indeed highly significant, especially when we consider that the entire framework of Roman Catholicism is based on the claim that Peter was Rome's first bishop!

It is claimed that Peter went to Rome about 41 A.D. and was martyred there in about 66 A.D. But there is not one bit of proof that Peter ever even went near Rome! Instead, the evidence is to the contrary. The New Testament tells us that Peter went to Antioch, to Samaria, to Joppa, to Caesarea, and other places, but *never* does it say he went to Rome! This is a strange ommission, especially when we remember that Rome was the Empire's capitol and was considered the most important city in the world!

Yet it is claimed that Peter suffered martyrdom there after a pontificate of 25 years. If we accept 66 A. D. as the date of his martyrdom, this would mean that he was bishop of Rome from 41 to 66 A. D. But about 44 A. D., he was in the Council at Jerusalem. (Acts 15). About 53 A. D., Paul joined him in Antioch. (Gal. 2:11) About 58 A. D., Paul wrote his letter to the Christians at Rome in which he sent greetings to twenty-seven persons, but never does he mention or greet Peter! Imagine a missionary writing to a

church, greeting 27 of the most prominent members, but never mentioning the pastor!

The accompanying photograph is a statue before which multiplied thousands have bowed. It is supposed to be a statue of Peter; but, as we shall see, it is actually an idol of non-Christian origin.

Since a study of the scriptures reveals that Peter was not the bishop of Rome, that he was not the first Pope, and that the Papal office was not instituted by Christ, what then is the real origin of the Papal office and the ideas that would attempt to link Peter with Rome? These things are all discussed in the chapter that follows.

79

CHAPTER ELEVEN

Pagan Origin of Papal Office

NIMROD, THE KING and founder of Babylon, was not only its political leader, but he stood as the priest-king, or its *religious* leader as well. From Nimrod descended a line of priest-kings—each standing at the HEAD of the occult Babylonian Mystery Religion. This line continued on down to the days of Belshazzar of whom we read in the Bible. Many are familiar with the feast he held in Babylon when the mysterious hand writing of doom appeared on the wall. Many have failed to recognize, however, that this gathering was more than a mere social party! It was a RELIGIOUS gathering. The filthy and abominable practices on the occasion were part of the religious ceremonies of the Babylonian Mysteries, of which Belshazzar was the head at that time! Says the Bible about this religious festival: "They drank wine, and praised the gods of gold, and of silver, and of brass, of iron, of wood, and of stone"(Daniel 5:4). Adding to the blasphemy of the occasion, they drank their wine from the holy vessels of the Lord which had been taken from the House of God! Such an attempt to MIX that which was holy with that which was heathenism, brought about God's swift judgment! Babylon was marked for doom!

In the course of time, the City of Babylon was completely destroyed. The ancient City is now in ruins, uninhabited, desolate (Jer. 50:39; 51:62). There is a railroad which runs from Baghdad to Basra which passes close to the old ruins. A sign written in English and Arabic says: "Babylon Halt, Trains stop here to pick up passengers." The only passengers, however, are tourists who come to inspect the ruins. But though the city was destroyed, concepts that were a part of the old Babylonian religion have continued to this day.

After Rome conquered the world, the paganism that had spread from Babylon and developed into various forms, was merged into the religious system of Rome, including the idea of a Supreme Pontiff or Pontifix Maximus. Thus, Babylonian paganism which had originally been carried out under the rulership of Nimrod, was united under the rulership of one man at Rome: Julius Caesar. It was the year 63 B.C. that Julius Caesar was officially recognized as the "Pontifix Maximus" of the Mystery Religion—now re-established at Rome. As is well known, this title and office was then held by each of the Roman emperors for many years.

To illustrate how this title was used by the Caesars, we show here an old Roman coin of Augustus Caesar (B.C. 27-14 A.D.) which shows his title as the "Pont-Max", that is, the Pontifix Maximus—the head of the pagan mysteries. (It is interesting to note that coins such as this were in circulation during the days of our Lord's earthly ministry: "And they brought unto him a penny. And he saith unto them, Whose is this image and super-scription? They say unto him, Caesar's"—Mt.22:17-22).

Other Roman emperors (including Constantine) continued to hold this office until 376 A.D. when the emperor Gratian, for Christian reasons, refused to be the "Pontifix Maximus" because he saw that such a title and office was idolatrous and blasphemous.

By this time, however, the bishop of Rome had arisen to political power and prestige. Did not many consider Rome the most important city of the world? Why then should not its bishop be "Bishop of bishops" and HEAD of the church? Thus many of the worldly minded religious leaders of this period reasoned. And so, as more and more compromises were made between Christianity and paganism, the bishop of Rome came into great prominence. Not only was he considered an important person by the fallen church, but because so much paganism had been mixed into the Romish church, he was also a man of acclaim to the pagans! Thus in 378, Demasus, bishop of Rome, was elected the "Pontifix Maximus"—the official High Priest of the Mysteries!

So clever was this mixture — this merger of paganism and Christianity—that ONE man was now looked to by BOTH pagans and professing Christians as HEAD! He was looked to by the "Church" as bishop of bishops; while the pagans regarded him as their Pontifix Maximus, whose office he actually held. By this time, and through the years that followed, the streams of paganism and Christianity flowed together, producing what is known as the Roman Catholic church, under the headship of the Supreme Pontiff or Pontifix Maximus—the Pope!

Even as the Caesars used the title "Pont. Max.", so have the Popes. The title is repeatedly found on inscriptions throughout the Vatican: above the entry of St. Peter's, above the statue of "Peter", in the dome, above the "Holy Year Door" which is opened only during a Jubilee year, etc. The accompanying medal, struck by Pope Leo X just before the Reformation, illustrates one of the ways that the title "Pont. Max." (Pontifix Maximus) has been used by the Popes. (Compare coin on page 81).

But how could a man be at one and the same time both the head of the church and still be the Pontifix Maximus, the head of the pagan Mysteries? In an attempt to cover this discrepancy, church leaders sought for similarities between the two religions. They knew that if they could find even a FEW points that both sides had in common, they could merge both into ONE—for by this time, the majority were not concerned about details... their desire was for *numbers* and *political power*. Truth was secondary.

One striking similarity that was found was this: The Supreme Pontiff of paganism bore the Chaldean (Babylonian) title פֶטֶר; that is, *peter*, or interpreter—the interpreter of the Mysteries![1] Here then was an opportunity for the compromising leaders of that time to "Christianize" the pagan office of "Pontifix Maximus", the office the bishop of Rome—the Pope—now held! By associating the "Peter", or Grand Interpreter of Rome, with Peter the Apostle (though there was no connection between the two whatsoever!), they could give the pagan office a *surface* appearance of Christianity.

But this presented its problems. To make the *apostle* Peter the *Peter-Roma* was difficult, for the "Peters" or "Interpreters" of the Mysteries, the Supreme Pontiffs, had from early times been connected with ROME! And so, in order to connect the apostle Peter with this pagan office—to make the merger less obvious—it was necessary to teach that the apostle Peter had gone to *Rome!* And this is the *real reason* that since the *fourth* century (and not before) that numerous tales began to be voiced in an attempt to prove that Peter went to Rome![2] And by teaching this, they were able to merge paganism and Christianity together under the headship of the Supreme Pontiff, the Father of fathers, or the Peter-Roma, the interpreter of the Mysteries at Rome! "And so, to the

1. Isis Unveiled, Vol. 2, p. 29; Parkhurst's Hebrew Lexicon, p. 602.
2. Hislop, p. 210.

blinded Christians of the apostasy, the Pope was the representative of Peter the apostle, while to the initiated pagans, he was only the representative of *peter*, the interpreter of their well-known Mysteries."[1]

Then other similarities were sought to associate Peter the apostle with the pagan office of Pontifix Maximus. One of these similarities had to do with *"keys."* For almost a thousand years before, the people of Rome had believed in the Mystic "keys"— the symbolic keys of the pagan god Janus and the goddess Cybele.[2] From olden times the "keys" had been symbols of the Mystery religion—in various forms and places. The Brahmatma, the supreme pontiff of India, for example, was regarded as the possessor of the "keys" and bore upon his tiara two crossed keys.[3] Mithraism, one of the main branches of the Mysteries that came to Rome, figured their sun-god Mithra as carrying two keys as the symbols of his authority.[4]

When all of this was absorbed into Rome, and the emperors claimed to be the successors of the "gods" and the Supreme Pontiffs of the Mysteries, the "keys" came to be the symbol of their authority also. Therefore, when the bishop of Rome, the Pope, became the Pontifix Maximus in about 378, he then became automatically the possessor of the Mystic "keys." This gained recognition for the Pope from the pagans; but how could this be associated with Christianity? Again apostate church leaders saw an opportunity to mix Peter into the story. Had not Christ said to Peter: "I will give unto thee the keys of the Kingdom of heaven" (Matt. 16:19)? However, it was not until 431 that the Pope publicly claimed that the keys he possessed were the keys of authority that had been given to the apostle Peter. This was over 50 years *after* the Pope had become the "Pontifix Maximus"—the possessor of the Keys! It is evident then that the keys that the Pope emblazons as the ensigns of his spiritual authority are those Mystic keys of paganism and not originally symbols of the keys Christ gave to Peter. (For one of many examples of how these keys are shown as the symbol of the Pope's authority, see the large fan on page 92).

Some have so *twisted* the scripture about Peter receiving the "keys of the kingdom", that many picture Peter as the gate keeper off up in heaven and that he decides who he will let in and who he won't! This is very much like the ideas that were associated with the pagan god JANUS, for he was the keeper of the doors and

1. Ibid.
2. Ibid, p. 207.
3. Isis Unveiled, p. 30.
4. Man and His Gods, p. 129.

gates in the pagan Mythology of Rome. Janus, with key in hand, is shown in the accompanying cut. He was represented with two faces —the one young looking, the other old (a later version of Nimrod incarnated in Tammuz).

The keys that our Lord gave to Peter were not literal keys to a literal door or gate. The key that was given to Peter (and to all the rest of the disciples that the Lord sent forth to preach) was the *message* of the gospel. And through this preaching of the gospel that was committed to them, men could be saved and become a part of the glorious Kingdom of God!

To go a little further, it is interesting to notice that not only were "keys" a symbol of Janus, but there was a bird that was "sacred" to him—the *cock*.[1] And even as the keys of Janus were adopted as symbols of the Pope and later associated with Peter, so the cock was also used in another attempt to harmonize pagan ideas with events in the life of Peter. Had not a COCK crowed on the night that Peter denied the Lord? (John 18:27). And so here was another similarity —a very vague one—but even this was used to make the pagan office of Pontifix Maximus, the High Priest of Janus, appear similar to that of Peter!

Now this title of "Supreme Pontiff" or "Pontifix Maximus" which the Pope bears, is obviously not a Christian designation, for it was borne by the pagan emperors of Rome before the Christian era. What was the significance of this title? As is well known, "pontiff" comes from the word *pons*, meaning "bridge", and *facio*, meaning "make." The word pontiff means "Bridge-builder." The priest-king emperors of pagan days were regarded as the makers and guardians of the bridges of Rome, to protect the city from invading armies. As High Priest of Roman religion in those pagan days, the title, drawing from its original meaning, had a religious significance: each of these priest-kings claimed to be the bridge or connecting link between this life and the next.

Obviously then, the title "Pontiff" had nothing to do with *true* Christianity! It was plainly the title of the pagan priest-kings. Yet the Popes continue to bear the title to this day. This fact alone

1. Encyclopedia of Religions, Vol. 2, Art. "Janus."

plainly shows how much influence paganism came to have in the "Church" at Rome.

The branch of the Babylonian Mysteries that came to Rome (by way of Persia) was known as Mithraism. Its influence grew in Rome until it became—at one time—almost the only faith of the empire.[1] In this branch of the Mysteries, the head priest was called the PATER PATRUM, that is, "The Father of the Fathers"! Borrowing directly from this title, at the head of the Roman Catholic religion is the PAPA, or Pope—the Father of the Fathers.[2] The "Father", or head of the Mysteries (just prior to the Christian era) had his seat at Rome; and so the "Father", or head of the Catholic church has his headquarters at Rome also!

In addition to this conclusive evidence, there is much more proof that the Pope is NOT the successor of the apostle Peter, but is instead, the successor of the line of High Priests of paganism —paganism that originated in Babylon: The expensive and highly decorated *garments* that the Popes wear indicate that the office of the Pope is of pagan origin, for such garments are patterned after those of the Roman emperors, not of the apostles! The historians have not let this fact go unnoticed, for indeed their testimony is that "the vestments of the clergy... were legacies from PAGAN Rome."[3]

The *tiara* that the Popes wear—though decorated in different ways at different times—is identical in *shape* to that worn by the "gods" or angels that are shown on ancient pagan Assyrian tablets.[4] (Cp. illustration at right with P. 96).

But the *Mitre,* worn by the Popes (and sometimes by Cardinals and Bishops), has an even more interesting origin, an origin that provides us with another clue in solving the identity of Modern Babylon today and the true origin of the Papal office! Such a mitre is shown in the illustration at the left, taken from the famous painting by Rubens of Theodosius and Ambrose (Fourth Century). Notice the *shape* of this headdress that Ambrose is wearing. There is certainly no indication that such a mitre was ever worn by

1. Ibid, p. 545.
2. The Paganism in Our Christianity, p. 145; Man and His Gods, p. 252.
3. The Story of Civilization, Vol. 4, p. 745.
4. Ancient Pagan and Modern Christian Symbolism, p. 63, 64.

Christ or the apostles! The mitre worn by Aaron and the Jewish high priests was entirely different than this, for that mitre was a turban. The type of mitre shown in our last illustration is unknown in the scriptures. From where then did this type of mitre that the Popes wear originate?

We will remember that the false "saviour" of Babylon in the "Mysteries" was represented in various ways and symbols. One of his mystery forms was as a FISH. In this form, Nimrod—Babylon's civilizer—was known as Oannes or as DAGON—*"Dag"* meaning "fish" and thus the "fish-god." The student of the scriptures will remember how hateful this pagan worship of Dagon was in the sight of God. Though it originated in the paganism of Babylon [1], Dagon worship became especially popular among the heathenistic Philistines. (Judges 16:21-30; First Samuel 5:5, 6). Old monuments often show Dagon represented as half man and half fish, as in the accompanying illustration.

Another way that Dagon, the fish-god, was depicted is seen in the illustration below (second figure from left). This is the way

he was pictured on Mesopotamian (Babylonian) sculptures.[2] And, as the noted Layard in "Babylon and Nineveh" has put it, "the head of the fish formed a MITRE above that of the man, while its scaly, fan-like tail fell as a cloak behind, leaving the human limbs and feet exposed."[3] Here then—in ancient times—was the use of the divided, somewhat pointed fish-head mitre, as though the jaws of the fish were slightly opened, the unmistakable counterpart of the mitre of the same shape that is worn by the Pope!

1. Encyclopedia of Religions, p. 502.
2. Ancient Pagan and Modern Christian Symbolism, p. 21.
3. Babylon and Nineveh, p. 343.

Later the fish body was removed and just the fish-head mitre was used to adorn the head of the great Mediatorial god. On several Maltese pagan coins, this god (whose characteristics are the same as those of Osiris, the Egyptian Nimrod!) is shown with the fish body removed, and only the fish-head mitre remaining.[1] (See illustration.) And

that such a mitre was used in the Babylonian worship is evident, for it is written that the Chaldean priests of Babylon also wore a head gear like a *fish's head!*[2] And it is this same type of pagan mitre that the Pope--the Pontiff of Babylon Modern—wears to this day. The mitre is seen in the accompanying sketch of Pope Paul as he delivered his serman on "peace" during his historic visit to the United States in 1965. (The photo on page 92 also shows the Pope wearing a highly decorated mitre of the same shape.)

As the noted writer Hislop puts it concerning the Papal mitre: "The two horned mitre, which the Pope wears when he sits on the high altar at Rome and receives the adoration of the Cardinals, is the very mitre worn by Dagon, the fish-god of the Philistines and Babylonians!"

A further identification between the Pope and ancient paganism may be seen in the *ring* which the Pope wears. H. A. Ironside says that the Pope is "the direct successor of the high priest of the Babylonian Mysteries and the servant of the fish-god Dagon, for whom he wears, like his idolatrous predecessors, the fisherman's ring." Now as we have seen over and over, in order to unite paganism and "Christianity" into one apostate church, leaders of the falling away constantly sought for similarities between the two systems. Whenever such similarities were found, the two sides could be merged in a much less obvious way. In this case, since Peter was at one time a FISHERMAN, the people were told

1. Two Babylons, p. 216.
2. Isis Unveiled, p. 485.

that this pagan fish-god ring, with the title "Pontifix Maximus" inscribed on it, was associated with the fisherman Peter. But such a ring was never worn by Peter the apostle. No one ever bowed and kissed *his* ring. He probably didn't even have a ring—for silver and gold he had none! (Acts 3).

Another clue to help us solve the mystery of Babylon Modern, may be seen in the use of the PALLIUM in the Roman Catholic church. A pallium, which the Pope wears over his shoulders, is shown in the accompanying illustration. The unabridged dictionaries define it as a garment that was worn by the PAGAN clergy of Greece and Rome, BEFORE the Christian era, and that it is worn today by the Pope on numerous occasions. Here  then is further proof of the paganism in the fallen church.

The pallium is made of white wool which is taken from two lambs which have been "blessed" in the basilica of St. Agnes, Rome. As a symbol that the archbishops also share in the plenitude of the Papal office, the Pope sends the pallium to them. However, before it is sent, it is laid all night on the supposed tomb of St. Peter—such a practice being a copy of paganism that was practiced among the Greeks!

A further attempt that was made to associate the Popes with  the Apostle Peter may be seen in the way the Roman church claimed to possess what they called the *Cathedra* of St. Peter —"Peter's Chair." (A sketch of this chair is shown in the accompanying illustration.) "The Romans had", says Bower, "as they thought, till the year 1662, a pregnant proof, not only of Peter's erecting their chair, but of his sitting in it himself; for, till that year, the very chair on which they believed, or would make others believe, he had sat, was shown and exposed to public adoration on...the festival of the said chair. But while it was cleaning, in order to set it up in some conspicious place of the Vatican, the 12 labours of *Hercules* unluckily appeared on it!"[1]

1. Bower's History of the Popes, Vol. 1, **p. 7.**

The Catholic Encyclopedia shows a photograph of this chair and mentions that the plates on the front of it show fabulous animals of Mythology as well as the fabled "Labours of Hercules."[1] Bearing in mind that the pagan carvings in connection with Hercules are on the chair, it is interesting to notice a statement made in another volumn of the Catholic Encyclopedia: "Gilgamesh, whom mythology transformed into a Babylonian Hercules... would then be the person designated by the Biblical Nemrod (Nimrod)."[2] In this statement, Nimrod is likened to Hercules and it is pagan carvings associated with Hercules that appear on the so-called "Chair of St. Peter." Considering these things, there is certainly no reason to believe that the chair originated in Christianity!

A scientific commission appointed by Pope Paul in July, 1968, has now reported that no part of the chair is old enough to date from the days of Peter. (By measuring the amount of radio-active carbon in wood, it can be determined how long ago a tree was cut). In the official report on the carbon dating and other tests, it has been proved that the chair is no older than the Ninth Century.

Many centuries ago a statue of the pagan god Jupiter was found in Rome. The large bronze statue in all its native ugliness was slightly altered and renamed as "St. Peter."[4] To this day, the statue is looked upon with the most profound veneration. In fact, the foot of this statue has been KISSED so many times by devotees, that the toes are nearly worn away![5]

The photograph on the next page shows a former Pope (John XXIII) about to kiss this statue. The statue was dressed up with rich papal robes and three-tiered papal crown for the occasion.

Now this practice of kissing an idol or statue is of PAGAN origin—the very paganism condemned by the Bible! As we have seen, BAAL worship was nothing more or less than the worship of the ancient Nimrod in deified form (as the sun-god). And the practice of kissing a statue of him was an ancient custom! What does the Bible say about it? In the days of Elijah, multitudes had bowed to Baal and KISSED him—the identical rite of which we are speaking. "Yet", God said, "I have left me seven thousand in Israel, all the knees which have not bowed unto Baal, and every mouth which hath not KISSED him" (1 Kings 19:18). Bowing and

1. Vol. 3, p. 554.
2. Art. "Babylon."
3. Isis Unveiled, p. 25 (note).
4. When the Emperor Leo in 628 published an edict against the use of religious pictures and statues in worship, the statue of Jupiter (renamed as Peter) was a special object of denounciation as evidenced by the letter that Pope Gregory wrote to Leo.
5. Ancient Monuments of Rome, p. 79.

kissing an idol then was a part of Baal worship!

In one of his "mystery" forms, Nimrod (incarnated in the young Tammuz) was represented as a calf. And so, in the Old Testament, when God's own people went after other gods, statues of calves were made, were worshipped, and KISSED! "They sin more and more, and have made them molten images of their silver, and idols according to their own understanding, all of it the work of the craftsmen: they say of them, Let the men that sacrifice KISS the calves"(Hosea 13:1-3).

And so we need not think it strange that along with other heathen practices that were absorbed into Catholicism, that *kissing an idol* has also become a part of the system! But to those who understand the "mystery", it is no longer a mystery at all! It becomes obvious that the very statue that was worshipped in pagan Rome as Jupiter (the Roman name and form of Tammuz) stands today, POSING as St. Peter, but the same old pagan worship and kissing of the idol continues—a sure indication of its paganistic origin! And little wonder it is that the Pope is also kissed on the foot, f o r he is in reality the representative—not of Christ or Peter the apostle —but of Babylonian religion!

Now even as such rites as kissing an idol were adopted into the Roman Catholic church, so also the custom of religious processions in which idols are *carried* was likewise adopted. Such processions are purely pagan in origin, yet they are a regular part of Catholic ceremonies. In the fifteenth century B. C. , an image of the Babylonian goddess Ishtar (Semiramis) was carried with great pomp and ceremony from Babylon to Egypt.[1] Such idol processions were practiced in Greece, Egypt, Ethiopia, Mexico, and many other pagan countries in olden times.

What does the BIBLE say about this practice? The Bible shows the folly of those who think good can come from idols—idols so powerless that they must be CARRIED! Isaiah, in direct reference to the gods of Babylon had this to say: "They lavish gold out of the bag, and weigh silver in the balance, and hire a goldsmith; and he maketh it a god: they *fall down*, yea, they *worship*. They bear him upon the *shoulder*, they *carry* him, and set him in his place, and he standeth; from his place shall he not remove" (Isaiah 46:6, 7)

Not only have such processions continued in the Roman Catholic church in which an IDOL is carried, but the POPE in like manner is also carried in procession. And even as the Bible tells us that the heathen in olden times lavished gold and silver on their god; so, such riches are placed on the Pope! And even as when the idol gods were carried in procession, the people would "fall down" and worship, so on certain occasions do people bow before the Pope as he is carried by. And even as men bore the idol god "upon the shoulders", so also men carry the Pope, the god of Catholicism, upon their shoulders in religious processions! (See photo on the next page!)

1. Hastings, Art., "Images and Idols."

But not only are such processions unscriptural, they are a continuation of ancient paganism.
Over three thousand years ago, the very *same* practice was known in Egypt, such processions being a part of the paganism there. The illustration at the right, shows the ancient Priest-king of Egypt being carried through worshipful crowds, borne by twelve men. A comparison of the Papal procession of today and the pagan procession of Egypt over three thousand years ago, shows that the one is a *copy* of the other!

We will also notice in the cut of the Egyptian priest-king, the use of the FABELLUM, a large fan made of feathers. This was later known as the "Mystic Fan of Bacchus." And even as this fan was carried in procession with the pagan priest-king, so also are these fans carried with the pope on state occasions. (Cp. cut with photo.) As the ENCYCLOPEDIA BRITANNICA says: "When going to solemn ceremonies, (the Pope) is carried on the sedia, a portable chair of red velvet with a high back, and escorted by two *fabelli* of feathers."[1] And that these processional fans originated in the paganism of Egypt is known and admitted even by Catholic writers.[2]

We see then how the pagan practice of processions, the main part being the carrying of the chair with the priest-king accompanied with the Mystic fans, has continued right on down to the present time in Babylon Modern—the Roman Catholic church. These things, the use of the pallium, the fish-head mitre, the "Babylonish garments", the Mystic "keys", the title "Pontiff" and the history of how the popes came to receive this title, all go together to provide *conclusive proof* that the PAPAL office is a PAGAN office. All of this, coupled with the fact that Christ never instituted any such office in HIS church, plainly shows that the Pope is not the Vicar of Christ or the successor of the Apostle Peter!

1. Vol. 22, Art., "Pope", p. 81.
2. The Popes—The History of How They Are Chosen, Elected, and Crowned, p. 108.

CHAPTER TWELVE

Papal Immorality

IN ADDITION TO the conclusive evidence that has been given, the very *character* and *morals* of many of the popes plainly show that they are not the successors of Christ or Peter, but successors of a pagan priesthood instead! Many of the Popes were so depraved and base in their actions, that even those who professed no religion at all were ashamed of them. Such sins as adultery, sodomy, simony, rape, murder, and drunkenness are among the sins that have been committed by popes. Now we know that to connect such sins with the men who have claimed to be the "Holy Father", the "Vicar of Christ", and the "Bishop of bishops", may sound shocking to some. But those who have studied the history of the popes well know that many of them were anything but holy men:

Pope Sergius III, who reigned from 904 to 911, obtained the papal office by murder. The annals of the church of Rome tell about his life of open sin with Marozia, a celebrated prostitute of the day, who bore him several illegitimate children.[1] This pope was described by Baronius and other ecclesiastical writers as a "monster" and by Gregorovius as a "terrorizing criminal." Says a historian: "For seven years this man... occupied the chair of St. Peter, while his concubine and her Semiramis-like mother held court with a pomp and voluptuousness that recalled the worse days of the ancient Empire."[2]

Now this woman—Theodora by name—that the historian likens to Semiramis (because of her corrupt morals), along with Marosia, the Pope's prostitute, "filled the papal chair with their paramours and bastard sons, and turned the Papal Palace into a den of robbers."[3] And so, beginning with the reign of Pope Sergius came the period (904-963) which is known as "The Rule of the Harlots."

1. The Priest, the Woman, and the Confessional, p. 138.
2. Medieval Italy, p. 331.
3. Halley's Bible Handbook, p. 774.

Theodora made John X pope (914-928). He had been sent to Ravanna as an Arch-bishop, but for her own lustful desires, she had him returned to Rome and appointed to the Papal office. His reign came to a sudden end when Marozia smothered him to death!

Marozia wanted John X out of the way, so she could raise Leo VI(928-929)to the office of Pope. His reign was a short one, however, for he was assassinated by Marozia when she learned that he had "given his heart to a more degraded woman than herself!"[1]

Not long after this, she raised her own illegitimate son by former Pope Sergius to the papal throne.[2] The boy was still in his teens! He took the name of John XI. But in quarreling with some of his mother's enemies, he was beaten and put into jail where he was poisoned and died.

In 955, the prostitute's grandson—after several bloody encounters—succeeded in taking possession of the Pontifical throne under the name of John XII. He became  so corrupt, that the Cardinals felt obligated to prefer charges against him. He refused to appear to answer the charges and threatened instead to excommunicate all of them! He was found guilty of various crimes and sins, including the following: He had put out the eyes of a high Catholic official who later died of the injuries. He set buildings on fire, drank a toast to the devil, played dice games in which he invoked the aid of demons, obtained money by unfair means, and was grossly immoral.[3] So vile were his actions, that even the noted Roman Catholic Bishop of Cremorne, Luitprand, said of him: "No honest lady dared to show herself in public, for Pope John had no respect either for single girls, married women, or widows—they were sure to be defiled by him, even on the tombs of the holy apostles, Peter and Paul."

He raised the ire of the people for turning the Lateran Palace into "a public whore house"[4], and was described by the Liber Pontificalis[5] with the words: "He spent his entire life in adultery." And finally, his life was ended while in the very act of adultery — killed by the woman's enraged husband.[6]

Pope Boniface VII (984-985) maintained his position through a lavish distribution of stolen money. The Bishop of Orleans, re-

1. The Priest, the Woman, and the Confessional, p. 138.
2. Annales Ecclesiastici, Vol. 15, p. 639.
3. The Other Side of Rome, p. 114.
4. Patrologine Latinae, Vol. 136, p. 900.
5. Vol. 2, p. 246.
6. Medieval Italy, p. 331, 336.

ferred to him (and also John XII and Leo VIII) as "monsters of guilt, reeking in blood and filth" and as "Anti-Christ sitting in the Temple of God." Besides these things, Boniface was a murderer. He caused Pope John XIV to be imprisoned and poisoned. When Pope John died, the people of Rome dragged his naked body through the streets. The bloody and shapeless mass that had been a pope was left to the dogs. The next morning, however, some priests secretly buried him.[1]

Boniface also murdered Pope Benedict VI, by strangling. Pope Sylvester II called him "a horrid monster surpassing all other mortals in wickedness."[2] But evidently Pope Sylvester was little better, for the Catholic Encyclopedia says that "the common people regarded him as a magician in league with the devil."[3]

Next came Pope John XV (985-996) who split the church's finances among his kinfolk[4] and earned for himself the reputation of being "covetous of filthy lucre and corrupt in all his acts."[5]

Benedict VIII (1012-1024) "bought the office of Pope with open bribery." The following Pope, John XIX (1024-1033) also bought the papacy and passed through all the necessary clerical degrees in one day! After this, Benedict IX (1033-1045) was made Pope as a boy 12 years old, through a money bargain with the powerful families that ruled Rome! He "committed murders and adulteries in broad daylight, robbed pilgrims on the graves of the martyrs, a hideous criminal, the people drove him out of Rome."[6]

Finally, simony—the buying and selling of the Papal office— became so common, and corruption so pronounced, that secular rulers stepped in. Henry III, emperor of Germany, appointed Clement II (1046-1047) to the office of Pope "because no Roman clergyman could be found who was free of the pollution of simony and fornication!"[7]

Many of the Popes were murderers, but no doubt Innocent III (1198-1216) surpassed all of his predessors in killing. During his reign, Innocent (not so innocently) had over a million so-called "heretics" murdered. He promoted the most infamous and devilish thing in human history—the INQUISIT- ION. For over five hundred years, Popes used the inquisition to maintain their power. Only God above knows how many people were killed because they did not agree with

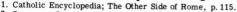

1. Catholic Encyclopedia; The Other Side of Rome, p. 115.
2. Sacrorum Conciliorium, Vol. 19, p. 132.   5. Annali d' Italia, Vol. 5, p. 498.
3. Vol. 14, p. 372.
4. Liber Pontificalis, Vol. 2, p. 246.   6. Medieval Italy, p. 349; Halley's Bible Handbook,
                                          7. Ibid.   p. 775.

everything taught by the Roman Catholic church.

Pope Boniface VIII (1294-1303) practiced sorcery.[1] He called Christ a "hypocrite", professed to be an atheist, denied life after death, was a murderer and a sex pervert. He is officially recorded as having said: "To enjoy oneself and to lie carnally with women or with boys is no more a sin than rubbing one's hands together."[2] Yet—and this sounds almost unbelievable—it was this Pope that wrote the infamous *"Unam Sanctum"* which officially declared that the Roman Catholic church is the one and *only* "true" church—outside of which no one can be saved! As immoral as he was, yet it was this Pope that also officially declared: "We, there-fore, assert, define and pronounce that it is necessary to salvation to believe that every human being is subject to the Pontiff of Rome."

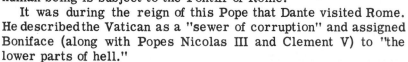

It was during the reign of this Pope that Dante visited Rome. He described the Vatican as a "sewer of corruption" and assigned Boniface (along with Popes Nicolas III and Clement V) to "the lower parts of hell."

Then from 1305 to 1377, the Papal Palace was at Avignon, France. During this time, Petrarch accused the Papal household of "rape, adultery, and all manner of fornication." And since the Popes were so immoral, it is no wonder that the priests were no better. Consequently, in many parishes men insisted on priests keeping concubines "as a protection for their own families!"[3]

During the Council of Constance, three popes, and sometimes four, were every morning cursing each other and calling their opponents Anti-Christs, demons, adulterers, sodomists, enemies of God and man. One of these "Popes", John XXIII (1410-1415 appeared before the Council to give account of his conduct. "He was accused by 37 witnesses (mostly bishops and priests) of forn-ication, adultery, incest, sodomy, simony, theft, and murder! It was proved by a legion of witnesses that he had seduced and violated 300 nuns. His own secretary, Niem, said that he had at Boulogne, kept a harem, where not less than 200 girls had been the victims of his lubricity."[4] All in all, the Council charged him with 54 crimes of the worse kind.[5]

Of this man, the official Vatican records offer this information

1. Durant, Vol. 6, p. 232.   4. The Priest, the Woman, and the Confessional, p. 139.
2. History of the Church Councils, Bk. 40, art. 697.
3. Halley's Bible Handbook, p. 778.   5. The Story of Civilization, Vol. 6, p. 10.

about his immoral reign: "His Lordship, Pope John, committed perversity with the wife of his brother, incest with Holy Nuns, intercourse with virgins, adultery with the married, and all sorts of sex crimes... wholly given to sleep and other carnal desires, totally adverse to the life and teaching of Christ... he was publicly called the DEVIL INCARNATE."[1] To increase his wealth, Pope John taxed about everything — including prostitution, gambling, and usury.[2] He has often been called "the most depraved criminal who ever sat on the papal throne."

Pope Pius II (1458-1464) was said to have been the father of many illegitimate children. He "spoke openly of the methods he used to seduce women, encouraged young men to, and even offered to instruct them in methods of, self-indulgence."[3] Pius was followed by Paul II (1464-1471) who maintained a house full of concubines. His papal tiara outweighed a palace in its worth.

Next came Pope Sixtus IV (1471-1484). Two illegitimate children were born to him by his mistress Theresia, which he made cardinals.[4] He financed his wars by selling church offices to the highest bidders[5] and "used the papacy to enrich himself and his relatives. He made eight of his nephews Cardinals, while as yet some of them were mere boys. In luxurious and lavish entertainment, he rivaled the Caesars. In wealth and pomp he and his relatives surpassed the old Roman families."[6]

Pope Innocent VIII (1484-1492) had 16 children by various women. He did not deny that these were his children, for their marriages were celebrated in the Vatican.[7] Like many other Popes, he multiplied church offices and sold them for vast sums of money. He permitted bull fights on St. Peter's square.

Next came Rodergio Borgia who took the name of Alexander VI (1492-1503) and won his election to the papacy by bribing the cardinals, a common practice of those days. Before becoming Pope, while a cardinal and archbishop, he lived in sin with a lady of Rome, Vanozza dei Catanei; and afterward, with her daughter Rosa, by whom he had five children. On his coronation day, he appointed his son—a youth of vile temper and habits—as Archbishop of Valencia.[8]

1. Sacrorum Conciliorum, Vol. 27, p. 663.
2. The Story of Civilization, Vol. 6, p. 10.
3. Halley's Bible Handbook, p. 779.
4. Annual of Universial Church History, vol. 2, p. 905.
5. Durant, vol. 6, p. 13.
6. Halley's Bible Handbook, p. 779.
7. Ibid.
8. History of the Reformation, p. 11.

Many consider Alexander VI to be the most corrupt of the Renaissance popes. He lived in public incest with his two sisters and his own daughter. He was both father and lover of his daughter, Lucretia, from whom—it is said—he got a child.[1]

On October 31, 1501, he conducted a sex orgy in the Vatican, the equal of which for sheer horror has never been duplicated—to say nothing of excelled—in the annals of human history.[2]

Concerning Pope Paul III (1534-1549), even pro-Catholic "Life" magazine said that as Cardinal he had fathered three sons and a daughter, and on the day of his coronation he celebrated the baptism of his two great-grandchildren; that he appointed two of his teenage nephews as cardinals; he sponsored festivals with singers, dancers, and jesters; and sought advice from astrologers.[3]

Pope Leo X (1513-1521) was appointed to 27 different church offices before he was 13 years old. He was taught to regard ecclesiastical offices purely as a source of revenue. He bargained for the papal chair and declared that the burning of heretics was a divine appointment.

During those days, Martin Luther, while still a priest of the papal church, journeyed to Rome. As he caught the first glimpse of the seven-hilled city, he fell to the ground and said: "Holy Rome, I salute thee." He had not spent much time in Rome, however, until he saw that Rome was anything but a holy city. He saw that iniquity existed among all classes of the clergy. Priests told indecent jokes and used awful profanity, even during mass. Luther later described the popes of that time as being worse in conduct than pagan emperors and told how the Papal court was served at supper by twelve naked girls.[4] "No one can imagine what sins and infamous actions are committed in Rome", he said, "they must be seen and heard to be believed. Thus they are in the habit of saying, 'If there is a hell, Rome is built over it'."[5]

One day during Luther's visit to Rome, he noticed a statue on one of the public streets that led to St. Peter's. The statue aroused his amazement, for it was a statue of a Pope, yet it was a woman! She was holding a sceptre, wore a papal mantle, and had an infant in her arms. Come to find out, this was a statue of the FEMALE pope! It was a statue of disgust to the Popes; consequently, no pope would ever pass down this certain street. "I am astonished," said Luther, "how the Popes allow the statue to remain."[6] Forty years after Luther's death, the statue was removed by Pope Sixtus V.[7]

1. The Priest, the Woman, and the Confessional, p. 139; The Rise and Fall of the Roman Catholic Church, p. 180.
2. Diarium, vol. 3, p. 167.
3. "Life" magazine, July 5, 1963.
4. Durant, vol. 6, p. 344
5. History of the Reformation, p. 56.
6. Ibid.   p. 59.
7. Ecumenicalism and Romanism,

But who was this female Pope that the statue represented? It is said that she was born in Rhineland, at Ingelheim. She won acclaim at Mainz for her learning. She later disguised as a man and entered the celebrated monastery of Fulda (between Frankfurt and Bebra). It is also said that she studied in England and at Athens and then received the position of a teacher in the *Schola Graecorum* at Rome, an ancient college for deacons. Here she gained so much influence, that when Pope Leo IV died, she—disguised as a man—was made Pope! However, after a pontificate of two years, one month, and four days, her sex was discovered! While taking part in a procession, she gave birth to an infant and died. And it was on this spot that the statue was erected of the female Pope.[1]

In recent times, the story of Pope Joan has been disputed. Rome, for obvious reasons, has tried to suppress it. However, before the days of the Reformation which exposed so much of the sin in the Romish church, the story was believed by chroniclers, bishops, and by Popes themselves![2] Pope Anastasius, for one example, mentions her in his "History of the Roman Pontiffs."[3] In fact, all text books before the Reformation mention Pope Joan either in the margin or in the text itself.[4] It is alleged that until the end of the fifteenth century, Popes had to undergo an examination lest again a *Papessa*—a female pope—should fill the Papal chair! Obviously, the idea of a female Pope does violence to the Catholic doctrine of "Apostolic succession" and so it is only natural that the Romish church should attempt to suppress the story.

As we come to the end of this chapter, having mentioned the gross immorality that has existed in the lives of some of the popes, we do not wish to leave the impression that ALL of the popes were as bad as the ones we have mentioned. No doubt these that have been mentioned are among the worst—if not the worst. But it has been necessary to mention these things to show the utter folly of the Catholic claim of the "Apostolic succession" of the Popes. For to make such a claim, each of these popes have to be included in the line—as wicked and immoral as some of them were! In attempting to trace this line back to Peter, even a female Pope would have to be included. And so the giant of Papal Succession to which ALL the claims of Romanism are attached, stands exposed as a fraud, and must fall before the mighty sword of the Spirit—the Word of God!

1. Medieval Italy, p. 392, etc.
2. Bower's History of the Popes, Vol. 1, p. 226.
3. P. 128, 1338
4. Ecumenicalism and Romanism, p. 59, 60.

CHAPTER THIRTEEN

Are Popes Infallible?

ADDING TO THE many contradictions with which the Romish system was already plagued, the Popes, like the god Janus of olden times, began to claim that they were "Infallible." But in view of the foregoing historical sketch, the idea of papal infallibility would immediately appear to be rank absurdity! Yet, most of the popes claimed to be infallible—infallible at least in pronouncing DOCTRINE, if not in morals and integrity. But this reasoning presented its problems. People naturally questioned: *How* could Popes be infallible in making doctrines, yet so utterly immoral in practice? But in spite of the inconsistency of the position, Papal infallibility was officially made a dogma in 1870.

Now the Pope that defined this doctrine of Infallibility was Pius IX (1846-78).[1] But he was certainly no example of infallibility —at least not in practice—for he had several mistresses (three of them nuns) by whom he had children. Nor was his predecessor, Pope Gregory XVI (1831-46) much better, for he was one of the greatest drunkards in Italy and he also had a number of mistresses, one of whom was the wife of his barber.[2]

Knowing the history of the Popes, several Catholic bishops were opposed to making the doctrine of Papal Infallibility a *dogma* at the Council of 1870. In speeches, several of them mentioned the apparent contradictions and immorality of the Popes. One such speech was given by Bishop Jose Strossmayer. In his argument against making "infallibility" a dogma, he mentioned how some of the Popes had opposed other popes, how they had contradicted each other, and made special mention of how Pope Steven brought former Pope Formosus to trial.

The famous story of one Pope bringing another to trial is one of sheer horror. You see, Pope Formosus had been *dead* for eight months! Nevertheless, his body was dragged from its tomb and brought to trial by Pope Steven. The dead, decaying body was carried in and proped upon the throne. There, before a group of bishops and Cardinals, was the body of the former Pope dressed

1. Encyclopedia Britannica, vol. 17, p. 224.
2. The Priest, the Woman, and the Confessional, p. 139.

in the rich apparel of the Papacy, a crown upon the loose scalp of his head and the scepter of the Holy Office placed in the stiff fingers of the rotting hand! As the trial got underway, the stench of the dead body filled the assembly hall.

Pope Steven stepped f o r w a r d and c l o s e l y questioned the dead man—the former Pope. Of course no answers were given to the charges; and so Pope For- mosus was p r o v e n guilty as charged! With this, the bright robes were ripped from the decaying body, the crown from his skull, the three fingers used in be- stowing the pontifical blessing were hack- ed off his decaying hand, and his body was thrown into the street. Behind a cart, the body was dragged through the streets of the city until finally it was cast into the Tiber River.[1]

Such actions—such sharp disagreement—between popes, cer- tainly does not sound like infallibility. Adding to the contradiction, after the death of Pope Steven, who had brought the dead body of Pope Formosus to trial and condemned him, the next Pope—Rom- anus—rehabilitated the memory of Formosus, as did also Pope John X. Obviously someone had to be wrong, for these Popes directly contradicted each other!

The fact is that neither in practice or in doctrine have the popes been infallible. Let us notice a few of the *hundreds* of con- tradictions to this doctrine of Papal Infallibility:

Pope Honorious I, after his death, was denounced as a heretic by the sixth Council in the year 680. Pope Leo confirmed his con- demnation. Now if Popes are infallible, how could one condemn another?

Pope Vigilius, after condemning certain books, removed his condemnation, afterward condemned them again and then retract- ed his condemnation, then condemned them again! Where is in- fallibility here?

Dueling was authorized by Pope Eugenius III (1145-53). But later Pope Julius II (1509) and Pope Pius IV (1506) forbade it.

In the Eleventh Century, there were three rival Popes at the same time, all of which were deposed by the council convened by the Emperor Henry III. Later in the same century, Clement III was opposed by Victor III and afterwards by Urban II. How could

1. The Rise and Fall of the Roman Catholic Church, p. 179; Medieval Italy, p. 395.

Popes be infallible when they opposed each other?

Then came the "great schism" in 1378 that lasted for fifty years. Italians elected Urban VI and the French Cardinals chose Clement VII. Popes cursed each other year after year, until a council deposed both and elected another!

Pope Sixtus V had a version of the Bible prepared which he declared to be authentic. Two years later Pope Clement VIII declared that it was full of errors and ordered another to be made!

Pope Gregory I repudiated the title of "Universal Bishop" as being "profane, superstitious, haughty, and invented by the first apostate."[1] Yet through the centuries, other popes have claimed this title. How then can we say that Popes are "infallible" in defining doctrine, if they directly contradict one another?

Pope Hadrian II (867-872) declared civil marriages to be valid, but Pope Pius VII (1800-1823) condemned them as invalid.

Pope Eugene IV (1431-1447), condemned Joan of Arc to be burned alive as a witch. Later, another Pope, Benedict IV, in 1919, declared her to be a "saint." Could this be papal infallibility?

How could all Popes be infallible when a number of Popes themselves denied such a teaching? Vigilinus, Innocent III, Clement IV, Gregory XI, Hadrian VI, and Paul IV all rejected the doctrine of Papal infallibility![2] Could an infallible Pope be infallible and not know it? Such inconsistency!

Considering the gross immorality, crookedness, and contradiction that has existed in the lives of many of the Popes, we can now see how blasphemous their claims really are! The Popes have taken to themselves such titles as "Most Holy Lord", "Chief of the Church in the World", "Sovereign Pontiff of Bishops", "High Priest", "The Mouth of Jesus Christ", "Vicar of Christ", and others. Said Pope Leo XIII, on June 20, 1894, "We hold upon the earth the place of God Almighty." And during the Vatican Council of 1870, on January 9, it was proclaimed: "The Pope is CHRIST in office, CHRIST in jurisdiction and power... we bow down before thy voice, O Pius, as before the voice of Christ, the God of truth; in clinging to thee, we cling to Christ."

But the historical sketch that we have given plainly shows that the Pope is NOT "Christ in office" or in any other way. We but have to compare the two—Christ and the Pope—and we have vivid proof that they are not in any way similar, but opposites!

The Pope wears a very expensive crown, covered with jewels. His triple decked crown is said to be worth $1,300,000. What a contrast this is to our Lord Jesus, who, during his earthly life wore no crown except the crown of thorns.

1. Epistola 5:20-7:33.   2. Roman Catholicism, p. 252.

The Pope is constantly waited on by servants. What a contrast to the lowly Nazarene who came not to be ministered to, but to minister!

The Pope's palace, extreme wealth, and luxury, stand in sharp contrast to the Lord Jesus who had nowhere to lay his head.

The Popes dress in garments that are very elaborate and costly—patterened after those of the Roman Emperors of pagan days. Such pride and vanity is contrasted to our Saviour who wore the gown of a peasant.

The immorality of many of the Popes stands in striking contrast to the Christ who is perfect in holiness and purity.

In view of these things, we can see that the claim that the Pope is the "Vicar of Christ" is without any basis in fact. But beyond this obvious contradiction, it is interesting to notice that the title "Filii Vicarivs Dei"—the Vicar of Christ—has a numerical value of exactly 666. This of course reminds us of the noted verse in Revelation 13:8: "Let him that hath understanding COUNT the number of the beast: for it is the number of a man; and his number is six hundred three score and six"—666.

In the title Vicar of Christ, "Filii Vicarivs Dei", the following letters have a numerical value in Latin: I equals 1, L equals 50, V equals 5, C equals 100, and D equals 500. (The remaining letters f-a-r-s-e have no numerical value.) The total of all the letters with numerical value in this title is 666.

The Pope and the Romish church are, of course, very closely associated in history—both ancient and modern—with ROME. According to Hislop, the original name of Rome was Saturnia, meaning "the city of Saturn" (Shobab Anishah) and Saturn was but another name for Nimrod! It was the secret name revealed only to the initiates of the Chaldean Mysteries, which—in Chaldee—was spelled with four letters—STUR. In this language, S is 60, T is 400, U is 6, R is 200, a total of 666.

Nero Caesar, one of the greatest persecutors of Christians and Emperor of Rome at the height of its power, has a name when written in Hebrew is "Neron Caesar" which also equals 666.

The Greek letters of "Lateinos"(Latin), the language of Rome in all its official acts, amount to 666! In the Greek, L is 30, A is 1, T is 300, E is 5, I is 10, N is 50, O is 70, S is 200. These figures total exactly 666. This same word also means "Latin Man" and is but the Greek form of the name ROMULUS, from which the present city of Rome is named! And—adding to the significance—this name in Hebrew, ROMIITH, also totals 666.

Unlike the Greeks and Hebrews, the Romans did not use all of their alphabet for numbers. They used only SIX letters: D, C, L, X, V, and I. (All other numbers were made up of combinations of these.[1]) It is interesting—and perhaps significant—to notice that the six letters that make up the ROMAN numeral system when added together total exactly 666!

D	500
C	100
L	50
X	10
V	5
I	1
total =	666

Turning to the Bible itself, in the Old Testament, we find that king Solomon each year received 666 talents of gold. (1 Kings 10: 14). This wealth played an important part in leading him astray.

In the New Testament, the letters of the Greek word "euporia," from which the word WEALTH is translated, total 666. Out of all the 2,000 Greek nouns of the New Testament, there is only one other word that has this numerical value and that word is "paradosis", translated TRADITION. (See Acts 19:25; Mt. 15:2). Wealth and tradition—strangly enough—were the two great corruptors of the Roman Church! Wealth corrupted in practice and honesty, and tradition corrupted in doctrine.

We are not here insisting on any dogmatic position as to this number 666, but we do believe these things show an interesting significance in connection with the words tradition, wealth, Latin, Rome, Roman numerals, and the Popes!

1. The "M" has now come to be used also as a Roman numeral representing 1000. But originally, 1000 was written as CI with another C turned around, that is, CIƆ. This was later simplified into ₥, and finally as M. See "Number in Scripture" by E. W. Bullinger, page 284.

CHAPTER FOURTEEN

The Inhuman Inquisition

SO OPENLY CORRUPT did the fallen "church" become in the middle ages, we can readily understand why in many sections of the land, men rose up in protest. Many were those noble souls who rejected the false claims of the fallen church and the Pope, looking instead to the Lord Jesus for salvation and to his Word for truth. These were called "heretics" and were bitterly persecuted by the Roman Catholic Church.

One of the documents that ordered such persecutions was the inhuman **AD EXSTIRPANDA** which was issued by Pope Innocent IV. This document stated that heretics were to be "crushed like venomous snakes." Priests, kings, and lay-members of the Romish system were called upon to join in the crusade. In so doing, said the document, any property they had gotten illegally would become rightfully theirs with a clear title and among other things, they were promised remission of all their sins if they killed a heretic!

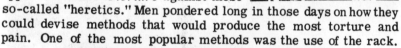

This Papal document also formally approved the use of *torture* against these so-called "heretics." Men pondered long in those days on how they could devise methods that would produce the most torture and pain. One of the most popular methods was the use of the rack.

This was a long table on which the accused was tied by the hands and feet, back down, and stretched by rope and windlass—thus dislocating the joints and causing great pain.

Heavy pincers were used to tear out fingernails or were applied red-hot to sensitive parts of the body; rollers with sharp knife blades and spikes attached were used, over which the "heretics" were rolled back and forth; there was the thumbscrew, an instrument made for disarticulating the fingers and "Spanish Boots" which were used to crush the legs and feet.

Then there was also the horrid "Iron Virgin", a hollow instrument the size and figure of a woman. Knives were arranged in such a way and under such pressure that the accused were lacerated in its deadly embrace. And what makes it even more blasphemous is that this and other torture devices were sprayed with "holy water" and inscribed with the latin words: "Soli Deo Gloria", meaning, "Glory be only to God." [1]

Victims, after being stripped of all their clothing, would have their arms tied behind their backs with a hard cord. Weights were attached to the feet. Then by action of a pulley, the victim would be suspended in mid-air. Then — as if this wasn't bad enough—the sufferer would be dropped and raised with a jerk, which dislocated the joints of his arms and legs. The cord by which he was suspended would penetrate the quivering flesh

1. Man and his Gods, p. 286.

to the bone. While such torture was being employed, priests holding up crosses would attempt to get the "heretic" to recant.

In the illustration below, taken from "Ridpath's History of the World"(Volumn 5), we see the work of the Inquisition in the Netherlands. Twenty-one protestants are hanging from the tree. The

man on the ladder is about to be hung. Standing below him is a priest holding up a cross, etc.

"In the year 1554 Francis Gamba, a Lombard, of the Protestant persuasion was apprehended and condemned to death by the sentence of Milan. At the place of execution, a monk presented a cross to him, to whom Gamba said, 'My mind is so full of the real merits and goodness of Christ that I want not a piece of *senseless stick* to put me in mind of Him.' For this expression, his tongue was bored through and he was afterwards burned."[1]

Others who rejected the teachings of the Roman church had molten lead poured into their ears and mouths. Eyes were gouged out and others were cruelly beaten with whips. Some were forced to jump from cliffs onto long spikes fixed below, where, quivering from pain, they slowly died. And still others were choked to death with mangled pieces of their own bodies, with urine, or excrement.

At night, the victims of the Inquisition were chained closely to the floor or wall where they were a helpless prey to the rats and vermin which populated those bloody torture chambers.

And not only were individuals and groups tortured and killed, but such also was the fate of entire *cities* which rejected the dogmas of Romanism. In 1209, for example, the city of Beziers was taken by men who had been promised by the Pope that by engaging

1. Foxe's Book of Martyrs, p. 103.

in the crusade against heretics they would immediately enter heaven upon death and that they would not even have to pass through purgatory to get there! Several Historians report that 60,000 in this city perished by the sword, while blood flowed in the streets.

At Lavaur in 1211, the governor was hanged on a gibbet and his wife thrown into a well and crushed with stones. Four hundred citizens of the town were burned alive. The Crusaders attended high mass in the morning, then proceeded to take other towns of the area where people had rejected the Catholic dogma. In this siege, it is estimated that 100,000 Albigenses (Protestants) fell in one day. Their bodies were heaped together and burned. The "clergy" thanked God for this great victory for the "church", and a hymn was composed and sung about this so-called victory.

Then there was the massacre of Merindol. Among other horrible things that transpired in this area that had become largely populated with Waldenses (Protestants), 500 women were locked in a barn which was set on fire. When any of them leaped from the windows, they were received on the points of spears! And, as in other cases, women were openly and pitifully violated. Children were murdered right before their parents who were powerless to protect them. Some were hurled from cliffs and others were stripped of all clothing and dragged through the streets.

Similar methods were used in the massacre of Orange in 1562. The Italian army was sent by Pope Pius IV and commanded to slay men, women, and children. The command was carried out with terrible cruelty, the people being exposed to shame and torture of every description.

Ten thousand Protestant Huguenots were killed in the bloody massacre in Paris on "St. Bartholomew's Day", 1572. The French King went to mass to return solemn thanks that so many of these "heretics" were slain. The Papal court received the news with great rejoicing and the Pope, Gregory XIII, in grand procession went to the church of St. Louis to give thanks for the victory! The Pope ordered the Papal mint to make coins commemorating the event. The coins showed an angel with sword in one hand and a cross in the other, before whom a band of Huguenots, with horror on their faces, were fleeing. Under the inscription are the words: *"Ugonottorum Strages 1572,"* which signify, "The slaughter of the Huguenots, 1572."

Even as late as the time of Napoleon, we read that after his troops had captured Toledo, an Inquisition prison was opened there. The historian of Napoleon's wars said it was like opening tombs, as the poor captives came forth. Their beards had grown down over their chests, their finger nails were like bird claws, and their bodies not much more than mere skeletons. Some of them had not breathed fresh air in years. Some were hopelessly crippled and deformed from having been kept in dens so low that they could not rise up in them. The next day, General LaSalle and several of his officers carefully inspected the place. The torture instruments they found filled even these men of the battlefield with horror.

The scene at the right shows the work of the Inquisition in Holland. A Protestant man is hanging by his feet in stocks. The fire is heating a poker to brand him and blind his eyes.

Now any one of the Popes could have stopped the horrible Inquisition by merely affixing his name and seal to a piece of paper. But did they? No. Some of the popes that today are acclaimed as "great" by the Romish Church, lived and thrived during those bloody days. Not one of them made a serious attempt to open the dungeon doors, to stop the slaughter of the dripping blades, or quench the murderous fires that blackened the skies of Europe for centuries!

And now I ask you: Could such a system that instituted this horrible Inquisition of the dark ages be the true church? Could a church that would employ such cruel methods be the Church founded by Him who said to turn the cheek, to forgive our enemies, to do good to them that despitefully use us? Who, even when hanging in death at the hands of evil men, said: "Father, forgive them, for they know not what they do"? Could these sadists—these monks and priests—be members of the pure, spotless, and undefiled bride of Christ? Or could their leader, the Pope of Rome, be the representative of that Christ on earth? I tell you NO, A MILLION TIMES NO!

110

CHAPTER FIFTEEN

"Lords Over God's Heritage"

THE HIGHEST ranking men of the Roman Catholic church, next to the Pope, are a group of men called "Cardinals." Now while our Lord did set apostles, prophets, evangelists, pastors, and teachers in his church (Eph. 4:11), never do we find any indication that he ordained a group of "Cardinals." What then is their origin?

As we study into this, it does not take long to discover that the Cardinals were a group of leading priests in the ANCIENT pagan religion of Rome—long *before* the Christian era. Later, when Christianity and Paganism were united at Rome—producing the Roman Catholic Church—the pagan office of the Cardinals was continued. The Cardinals are not the successors of the apostles, but instead they are the successors of the pagan priests of ancient Babylon by way of Rome!

In the booklet "This is the Catholic Church", published by the Knights of Columbus (a Catholic lay-organization), we read: "In ancient times the cardinals were the chief clergy of Rome—the word is derived from the Latin word *cardo*, 'hinge', and thus referred to those who were the pivotal members of the clergy."[1] And so it is admitted—by the Catholic church itself—that the cardinals were originally the leaders of the pagan clergy of ancient Rome, the priests of the Hinge.

But just who were these priests of the Hinge? With just a little further study, we find unmistakable evidence that these priests of the hinge were the priests of Janus, the pagan god of doors and HINGES! As the god of doors and hinges, Janus was referred to as "the god of beginnings"—thus January, the beginning month of our Roman Calendar, comes from his name. Janus was believed to be the protector or caretaker of the doors. Even today, the keeper of the doors is still called a JANITOR, a word that is taken from the name of Janus![2]

As keeper of the doors, Janus was known as "the opener and

1. This is the Catholic Church, Booklet 50, p. 38.
2. Story of the World's Worship, p. 180.

shutter."[1] Since the worship of this false god, "the opener and shutter", was very strong in Asia Minor, we can understand why Jesus speaking to the church at Philadelphia said: "These things saith he that is holy, he that is true, he that hath the key of David, he that openeth and no man shutteth: and shutteth, and no man openeth...I have set before you an OPEN DOOR"(Rev. 3:7, 8). The pagan god Janus was a counterfeit! JESUS is the *true* opener and shutter!

When paganism and Christianity were mixed together at Rome, the college of Cardinals—priests of the Hinge, the clergy of Janus —that had served Pagan Rome, soon found a place in Papal Rome! And thus, the office of cardinals—as unscriptural as it is—entered the professing church and has continued to this day. But why did ecclesiastical leaders allow this pagan order of Cardinals to find a place in the "church"? The answer is obvious. By mixing such paganism into Christianity, both professing Christians and pagans could be united. And thus—by such mixtures—the Roman Catholic Church was formed and prospered.

But even before the days of Papal *or* Pagan Rome, even back in the days of Babylon, a similar order of high priests was known. "The college of Cardinals, with the Pope at its head", says Hislop, "is just the counterpart of the pagan college of Pontiffs, with its Pontifex Maximus, or Sovereign Pontiff, which is known to have been framed on the model of the grand original Council of Pontiffs at Babylon!"[2]

Besides this evidence of the pagan origin of the office of the Cardinals, there is more proof—striking proof—to be found even in the colours of the garments that they wear! As is well known, the garments worn by the Cardinals of the Catholic Church are *red* in color. This fact has been so long established, that a cardinal bird and cardinal flower, which are both red in color, get their names from the Cardinals who are also adorned in red. But originally this color was a color typifying sin, as was mentioned even back in the days of the Prophet Isaiah: "Though your sins be as scarlet, they shall be white as snow, though they be red like crimson, they shall be as wool"(Is. 1:18). And right on down to the present day, red has continued to be a color associated with sin, with prostitution, etc. In like manner, when the Bible symbolized the religion of Babylon under the figure of an ill-famed woman, a whore, she was dressed in scarlet-red garments.

Now turning to Ezekiel 23, in the parable of Aholah and Aholibah, reference is made to a group of men of ancient Babylon dressed

1. Fasti, p. 130.
2. Two Babylons, p. 206.

112

in bright red garments! "...For when she saw men pourtrayed upon the wall, the images of the Chaldeans pourtrayed with VERMILLION"—bright red!—"girded with girdles upon their loins, exceeding in dyed attire upon their heads, all of them princes to look to, after the manner of the BABYLONIANS of Chaldea, the land of their nativity"(Ez. 23:14, 15). Here then is special mention made of certain princes of Babylonian origin who were distinctively dressed in bright red garments.

Now these same red garments were worn by the "priests of the hinge"—the cardinals of pagan Rome—who were also known as the FLAMENS. This title was taken from the word flare, meaning one who blows or kindles the sacred fire.[1] They were the keepers of the holy "flame" which they fanned with the "Mystic fan" of Bacchus. And like the color of the fire they tended, their garments were flame colored—bright red. And so to this day, the Cardinals wear garments of the same color. The Flamens were servants of the Pontifex Maximus in pagan days and the Cardinals are the servants of the Pope who also claims the title of Pontifex Maximus. The Flamens were divided into three distinct groups, so also today the Cardinals are divided into three different groups—Cardinal Bishops, Cardinal Priests, and Cardinal Deacons.

The origin then of the Catholic Cardinals seems definitely connected with ancient paganism, as evidenced by the very title they carry (priests of the Hinge), by the fact that such an office was never instituted by Christ, and by the very color of their garments!

Next in authority under the Pope and the Cardinals are the *bishops* of the Catholic Church. Unlike the office of the Pope and the Cardinals, however, the scriptures do mention the office of bishops. But the *scriptural* teaching concerning bishops is quite *different* from the Roman Catholic position.

Romanism has so influenced the thinking of the people in this respect that it is commonly believed that the office of a bishop is a different and much *higher* office than that of the ministers of a local church. Have not most of us assumed that a bishop has authority over a group of churches and ministers?

But what saith the scriptures? The Bible plainly shows that EVERY minister of the local church is a BISHOP! There is absolutely *no difference* between the elders of the church and the bishops—both are the same.[2] Consider the following evidence from the scriptures on this point:

1. Harper's Dictionary of Classical Literature and Antiquities, p. 675.
2. See Scofield Bible, p. 1283 (note).

Paul instructed Titus: "Ordain elders in EVERY city, as I had appointed thee"(Titus 1:5). Then Paul went ahead to explain the qualifications of these elders and explained that an elder is a "bishop"(Verse 7). Plainly, the elders of each local church—in *every* city—were bishops. This is quite different from the commonly assumed idea that a bishop bears rule over a group of churches or less important ministers!

In connection with this, it is interesting to notice that the word "Cathedral" comes from the word *Cathedra* which means *throne*, for a Cathedral is a large church in a large city where the throne of the bishop is located. (See Dictionary). Obviously, this idea is quite contrary to the teaching of Paul that bishops were to be ordained in "every city" and that the elders or ministers of the local church and bishops are all one and the same!

This truth is also seen in Acts 20. In this chapter, Paul "sent to Ephesus, and called the ELDERS of the church"(Verse 17). Then in speaking to these elders, he said: "Take heed therefore unto yourselves, and to the flock over which the Holy Ghost hath made you OVERSEERS (bishops)"(Verse 28). The word here translated "overseers" is exactly the same word that is elsewhere translated bishops! So again we see that elders and bishops are the same. Paul then exhorted these elders of Ephesus "to FEED"(Greek, *"pastor"*) "the church of God, which he hath purchased with his own blood..."(Verse 28). These elders from Ephesus then were referred to as elders, bishops, overseers, and pastors—all of these expressions referring to exactly the SAME office. These men were the ministers of the local church! Plainly enough then, a bishop—in the scriptures—was not a minister of a large city who sat on a throne and exercised authority over a group of churches or other ministers. Each church had its elders and these elders were bishops!

Martin Luther understood that the elders and bishops in the early true church held exactly the same office. "But as for the bishops that we now have," he remarked, "of these the Scriptures know nothing; they were instituted... so that one might rule over many ministers..."[2]

As the falling away came, even as other departures from the faith were made, so the true pattern for church *government* was also sadly neglected as men substituted *their* ideas. Men began to exalt themselves as "lords" over God's heritage. Even before our New Testament was completed, we find that in Asia the false doctrine of the Nicolaitanes was creeping in. According to Scofield,

1. To the German Nobility (Harvard Classic), p. 317.

the word Nicolatines come from *nikao*, "to conquer", and *laos*, "the people" or "laity." He says further: "If the word is symbolic it refers to the earliest form of the notion of a priestly order, or 'clergy', which later divided an equal brotherhood(Mt. 23:8), into 'priests' and 'laity'."[1] And so the basic idea of men exalting themselves above others, crept in and has continued in the fallen church to this day.

Often ministers are referred to as the "clergy" and the other members as the "laity." The common conception is that the "clergy" are on a somewhat higher plain. Consequently, there is probably only one in a thousand that knows that the term "clergy" belongs to EVERY humble Christian believer, not just to ecclesiastical leaders. Notice that 1 Peter 5:1-3 instructs ministers not to be "lords over God's heritage." The word here translated "heritage", in the original, is "Kleeron" which means "clergy"! The Matthew Henry commentary explains that *all* the children of God are given the "title of God's heritage, or *clergy*...the word is never restrained in the New Testament to the ministers of religion only." [2]

But men desiring positions of dignity departed from the scriptural plan for church government. Finally men were taught that they needed a priest to whom they would tell their sins; a priest must sprinkle them; a priest must give them the last rites; a priest must say masses for them, etc. Thus, the people were taught to depend upon a human priest, while the true high priest, the Lord Jesus, was obscured from the view of the people by a dark cloud of man-made traditions.

Then rising above these priests, certain men claimed to be bishops—rulers over other churches and ministers—as we have just seen. And finally the idea of a Bishop of bishops—as a further step into apostasy—was adopted into the *fallen* church! But, as we have seen earlier, no where do the scriptures teach that ONE man was to be head of the church, other than THE man, Christ Jesus! Nor do the scriptures teach that one man was to be head over a group of ministers—in the way Catholic bishops are today. And to go a step further, there is no where in the New Testament where ONE man was to have all the authority over a local church. Instead, all New Testament churches were pastored by a PLUR-ALTY of ministers or elders! Never was the full guidance of a church placed in the hands of only *one* individual. The person on whom everything depended might acquire too great an importance, become the center, and obscure the common relation that

1. Scofield, p. 1332 (note).   2. See Barnes, etc.

115

all brethern have to the one, CHRIST, the Lord!

When Barnabas and Paul had completed a tour through a number of places, we are told that "they ordained them ELDERS (plural) in every church"(Acts 14:19-23). While at Miletus, Paul "sent to Ephesus and called the ELDERS (plural) of the church"(Acts 20: 17). The letter to the Phillippians is addressed "to all the saints in Christ Jesus who are at Philippi, with the BISHOPS (Elders— plural)"(Phil. 1:1). To the church at Thessalonica it was written: "We beseech you, brethern to know THEM (plural) who labour among you, and are over you in the Lord, and admonish you"(1 Thess. 5:12). Titus was to "ordain ELDERS (plural) in every city" (Titus 1:5). The activities of the church at Jerusalem were carried on by "ELDERS"(plural). (Acts 15:1, 2). And those who were sick were instructed to "call for the ELDERS (plural) of the church" for prayer and healing. (James 5:14, 15). So clearly taught in the scriptures is this pattern, it is hard to understand why so much of professing Christendom ever departed from it.

As the leaders of the "falling away" instituted positions in which men could be "lords" over the church, they also adopted equally unscriptural *titles* to designate these positions. Unlike Job of old who did not want to "give flattering titles unto man"(Job 32:21), apostate church leaders began to set themselves up in varying positions of unscriptural authority in the "church" and took to themselves titles that scripturally belong only to God—DIVINE titles.

Concerning such titles, our saviour taught: "Be not ye called Rabbi: for one is your Master, even Christ; and all ye are brethern. And call no man your father upon the earth: for one is your Father, which is in heaven. Neither be ye called masters: for one is your Master, even Christ. But he that is greatest among you shall be your servant. And whosoever shall exalt himself shall be abased; and he that shall humble himself shall be exalted"(Mt. 23:8-12).

It is pitiful to think that a church that *claimed* to have Christ as its founder—after a few centuries—began to use the very titles that Christ told us NOT to use! But this is how far the "church" departed from the faith. In many things they did just the OPPOSITE of what Christ and his apostles taught. As these times of the falling away came, the bishop of Rome began to exalt himself (as we have seen) and took to himself the blasphemous title of "Pope", which is just another variation of "Father", the very title that Christ told us not to apply to any religious leader!

116

And even though Christ told us to "call no man father", yet to this day the priests of Catholicism insist on this title! Christ forbade the use of this title, for it is a *divine* title which, in the religious sense, should be applied only to God. The practice of applying it to a religious leader originated in paganism. We will remember that one of the leading branches of the "Mysteries" that came to Rome in the early days was Mithraism. And in the Mithraic Liturgy, those who presided over the sacred ceremonies were called "fathers."[1]

And that this title of "father" was used in connection with priests in olden times is mentioned in the Bible itself. In Judges 17, we read about a man named Micah who said to a young Levite man: "Dwell with me, and be unto me a FATHER AND A PRIEST" (Judges 17:10). Now Micah was a grown man with a son of his own, whereas the Levite was "a *young* man." Certainly then the term "father" was not used in the sense of respect for an older man, nor was Micah the fleshly, literal father of the young man. There is only one sense then in which the title "father" was used. It was used as a religious title, a priestly designation. Micah wanted him to be a father-priest in his "house of gods."

Then in Chapter 18 of the book of Judges, the young man was asked to serve a whole tribe as its father-priest! "Be to us a FATHER and a PRIEST: is it better for thee to be a priest unto the house of one man, or that thou be a priest unto a tribe and a family in Israel?" A study of these two chapters shows a type of Catholicism in the Old Testament. For while the priest claimed to speak the word of the "LORD"(Judges 18:6), yet the worship was that of idols and paganism—an attempt to mix both heathenism and the worship of God into one! And such "mixing" has always brought about the displeasure of the Lord.

Certainly then, a priesthood that insists on using a pagan and pre-Christian title which the Lord Jesus himself expressly told us *not* to use, cannot be a Christian priesthood!

Other church leaders of the Roman Catholic system carry the title of Monsignor, which is not only unscriptural, but having the meaning of "my lord"[2], is in direct disobedience to the scripture that says ministers are not to be "lords" over God's heritage! The use of such titles is contrary to what Christ taught, for in direct reference to flattering religious titles, he said: "Whosoever shall exalt himself shall be abased."

Jesus also told the disciples not to be called "Masters." This too is a DIVINE title rightly belonging only to our saviour. As

1. Mysteries of Mithra, p. 167.
2. This is the Catholic Church, p. 38.

Jesus said: "For one is your master, even Christ." Now at first glance, we may not think that this title has been used in Catholicism —the fallen church—but a closer look reveals that it has. For example, such titles as Archbishop, Archpriest, Archdeacon, all carry this meaning. You see, one of the meanings of "Arch" is MASTER! And so to put this in front of a title like "Archpriest" would give it the meaning of Master-priest, etc.

Now the awakening that came in the days of the Reformation, rejected these blasphemous titles of Pope, Cardinal, Monsignor, and others. Unfortunately, however, it retained other titles from Catholicism that were just as unscriptural. And so to this day, in both the Catholic and most of the Protestant churches, the unscriptural title of *"Reverend"* has continued to be used, for example. Variations of this are: Reverend, The Reverend, The Very Reverend, The Most Reverend, and the Right Reverend. But never were such titles applied to the ministers of the early church! (As a minister of the gospel, I do not use the title "Reverend" in any form in front of my name.) That there are fine ministers that use this title, we do not deny; but most of them do so merely from tradition, never actually questioning its original significance.

Titles such as Master or Father were condemned by Christ, because these are titles that—in the spiritual sense—belong only to God. And on the *same* basis, the title "Reverend" in its various forms should also be rejected; for, in scriptural usage, the title is applied *only* to God. As we read in Psalms 111:9, "Holy and REVEREND is HIS name."

Would it not be better to stay right with the scriptures and use the expressions it uses? Should we not reject the supposed "authority" of those high offices in which men seek to make themselves "lords over God's heritage"? And instead of men receiving the glory, should not all the glory be given to God?

CHAPTER SIXTEEN

An Unmarried Priesthood

THE SPIRIT SPEAKETH expressly, that in the latter times, some shall depart from the faith, giving heed to seducing spirits, and doctrines of devils; speaking lies in hyprocrisy; having their conscience seared with a hot iron; FORBIDDING TO MARRY..."(1 Timothy 4:1-3).

From this passage, we know that a departure from the true faith was prophesied by the apostle Paul. He mentioned that this would occur in "latter times"; that is, *later* times from the time that he was writing. The departure would not happen all at once, but in later *"times"* (plural), little by little, would men go into apostasy—departing from the true faith and giving heed to "doctrines of devils."

Now these doctrines of devils were the teachings of the pagan Mysteries. (It is evident that Satan and his demon hosts were behind the pagan teachings—the Mysteries—for they contained many similarities, counterfits, and parallels with truth.) And in the above passage, special mention is made of one of these pagan doctrines—the doctrine of "forbidding to marry." But *what* was this doctrine and *to whom* did it apply?

As we study into this, we find that the pagan doctrine of "forbidding to marry" did not apply to everyone. It was a doctrine held from ancient times in connection with the PRIESTS of the Mysteries, the religion of Babylon! Yes, way back in the early days of Babylon, among other doctrines of devils that were held, was the doctrine of priestly celibacy. These unmarried priests were members of the higher orders of the priesthood of Queen Semiramis who bound them to a life of celibacy, though Semiramis, herself, was a very immoral and adulterous woman. "Strange as it may seem", writes Hislop, "Yet the voice of antiquity assigns to the abandoned queen the invention of clerical celibacy, and that in its most stringent form."[1]

From Babylon this doctrine of an unmarried priesthood spread to other nations—as evidenced by the celibate priests of religions

1. Two Babylons, p. 219.

in Thibet, China, Japan, and other countries. However, some nations, while strictly holding to other parts of the Mystery religion, did not always enforce the rule of celibacy, as in Egypt where priests were allowed to marry. BUT, when the Mysteries came to Rome in pre-Christian times, the rule of celibacy was strictly observed!

"Every scholar knows," says Hislop, "that when the worship of Cybele, the Babylonian Goddess, was introduced into Pagan Rome, it was introduced in its primitive form, with its celibate clergy."[1] And so, this doctrine of devils—that priests must be unmarried—became established in pagan Rome. But instead of priestly celibacy resulting in PURITY to those intangled therein, the opposite has *always* been the result. Especially was this true of the celibate priests of Pagan Rome. The excesses they committed were so bad that the Senate felt they should be expelled from the Roman Republic.

But as the days of the departure from the true faith came, in spite of the corrupt fruits this system of celibacy had produced in pagan Rome, even this doctrine of "forbidding to marry" became a part of PAPAL Rome—the Roman Catholic Church! Such a compromise with paganism shows the depths men will go to attain numbers and position. By adopting this doctrine into the Romish "church", they wilfully denied the plain teachings of the Bible. The Bible never set forth any rule that a minister must be an unmarried man. Ministers of the New Testament church, including apostles, were married men (1 Cor. 9:5). The Bible says: "A bishop then must be blameless, the husband of one wife"(1 Tim. 3:2).

And even as corruptions existed among those celibate priests in ancient times and in pagan Rome, so also did corruption continue among the priests of papal R o m e. For example, "When Pope Paul V meditated the supression of the licensed brothels in the 'Holy City', the Roman Senate petitioned against his carrying his design into effect, on the ground that the existence of such places was the only means of hindering the priests from seducing their wives and daughters."[2]

Rome, during those days, was a "holy city" in name only. Reports estimate t h a t there were about 6,000 prostitutes in this city with a population not exceeding 100,000.[3] Historians tell us that "all the ecclesiastics had mistresses, and all the convents of the Capitol were houses of bad fame." A fish pond at Rome which was situated near a convent was drained by order of Pope Gregory and lo! at the bottom were found over 6,000 infant skulls.

1. Ibid, p.220.   3. Durant, Vol.6, p.21.
2. Ibid.   4 History of the Reformation, p.

When the foundations of the nunnery at Neinburg, Austria, were searched, the same results of celibacy were found![1] Such was also the case when various g a r d e n s and subterranean vaults of convents in Italy were searched.[2]

Cardinal Peter d'Ailly said he dared not describe the immorality of the nunneries, and t h a t "taking the veil" w a s simply another mode of becoming a public prostitute. Violations were so bad in the ninth century that St. Theodore Studita forbade even female animals on monastery property!

In the year 1477, night dances and orgies were held in the Catholic cloister at Kercheim that are described in history as being worse than those to be seen in the public house of prostitution.[3] Priests came to be known as "the husbands of all the women." One Catholic bishop in Germany began to charge the priests in his district a tax for each female they kept and each child that was born. He discovered that there were ELEVEN THOUSAND women kept by the clergymen of his diocese![4] A l b e r t the Magnificent, Archbishop of Hamburg, exhorted his c l e r g y: "Si non caste, tamen caute"(If you can't be chaste, at least be careful).

While it is true that there have been cases in which married ministers—of various churches and religions—have fallen into immorality, such cases have been the *exception*, not the rule. But in the case of the unmarried priesthood of Papal Rome, especially during the Middles Ages, such immoral conduct became the *rule!*

Taking all of these things that we have mentioned into consideration, we can see how EXACTLY the prophecy of 1 Timothy 4: 1-3 was fulfilled. The prophecy given by Paul said there would be a departure from the faith; people would come to believe doctrines of devils; they would forbid to marry; would sear their consciences; and speak lies in hypocrisy. Did the departure from the true faith come? Yes! Did people give heed to pagan doctrines, the doctrines of devils? Yes! One of these doctrines—as we have seen—was the doctrine of forbidding priests to marry. Was this doctrine believed by those who departed from the true faith? Yes! These priests—while they were supposed to be holy men—were often just the opposite, as the result of the celibacy doctrine. Thus, their "consciences were seared with a hot iron" and by the lives they led, they "spoke lies in hyprocrisy."

The prophecy was exactly fulfilled!

Further evidence that identifies the doctrine of celibacy and

1. Isis Unveiled, p. 58.
2. Ibid, p. 210.
3. The Decline of the Medieval Church, p. 295.
4. History of the Reformation, p. 11.

its resulting immorality with that of paganism is seen in the use of the CONFESSIONAL. As we shall see, the confessional was used in many heathen lands, including Babylon. But wherever and whenever it has been used, the results have not been of purity, but of corruption.

In the confessional, young girls and women confess their moral weaknesses and desires, and often unmarried priests have thus chosen their victims. A full account of such corruption in connection with the confessional, along with actual cases, is given in a book written by an ex-priest himself— "The Priest, Women, and Confessional." These things are also brought out in the book "Crime and Immorality in the Catholic Church", by ex-priest Emmett McLoughlin.

"But", some may question, "Does not the Bible say we are to confess our faults one to another?" Yes, there is a type of confession that is taught in the scriptures, but it is *not* confessing to an unmarried priest! The Bible says: "Confess your faults ONE TO ANOTHER" (James 5:16). If this scripture could be used to support the Catholic idea of confession, then not only should the people confess to the priests, but the priests should confess to the people! Obviously, the teaching of Romanism is contrary to the scriptural admonition of confession "one to another." But insisting that the people tell their sins to a priest, the people are bound to a human priest who may, in many cases, be a greater sinner than themselves! And so securely are Roman Catholics bound to the human priest and the confessional, they believe that their very salvation is dependent upon such confession!

But no one in the New Testament ever obtained forgiveness from a priest. Peter told Simon Magus to "pray to God" for forgiveness (Acts 8:22). This is quite significant, especially when so many have been taught that Peter was the Pope, the Bishop of bishops! Yet Peter did not tell this man to confess to him. Nor did Peter tell him to do penance—like saying the "Hail Mary" for a given number of times a day for a certain period of time. It is also significant to notice that when Peter sinned, he confessed his sin to *Christ* and was forgiven. But when Judas sinned, he confessed his sins to the priests and committed suicide!(Mt. 26: 75; 27:1-5).

The practice of confessing to a priest came not from the BIBLE, but from BABYLON! Queen Semiramis created such confession as part of the "Mysteries" and secret confession to a priest was required before complete initiation was granted. Once such confession was made, the victim was henceforth bound hand and foot to the priesthood. That such confession took place in Babylon is well known by *every* historian who has written of the religion of that ancient land. For indeed, our knowledge of the Babylonian idea of SIN, comes not from comprehensive lists of sins, but from certain confessions that were made in which sins were enumerated in the confession ritual! And from such recorded confessions—and ONLY from these—have historians been able to draw their conclusions about the Babylonian concept of wrong.[1]

From Babylon, the "Mother", this scheme later permeated all the religions of the world. Salverte wrote of this practice among the Greeks in these words: "All the Greeks from Delphi to Thermopylae, were initiated in the mysteries of the temple of Delphi. Their silence in regard to everything they were commanded to keep secret was secured by the general CONFESSION exacted of the aspirants after initiation..." Such was also a part of the religions of Medo-Persia, Egypt, and Rome—before the Christian era ever dawned. And so by seeing the heathenistic origin and history of confession to a priest, provides us with another point of identification toward understanding the "Mystery" of Babylon in our times!

Beyond this, we see an interesting significance also in the *color* of the priestly clergy garments. As is well known, Catholic priests wear BLACK garments and some Protestant denominations have also adopted the practice. It is a wide-spread and well established custom. But how did it originate?

Turning to the scriptures, we find absolutely no evidence that the ministers all wore some distinctive color of garments. Surely there is nothing to indicate that the Lord Jesus wore BLACK clergy garments nor is there any indication that the apostles of the early church were required to dress in this color.

Black, on the other hand, has for many centuries been a sign of DEATH. Hearses are black, black is worn by mourners at a funeral, and in numerous ways is associated with death. Consid-

1. The Greatness that was Babylon, p. 268.

ering that this is the color that priests are required to wear—the color that is symbolic of death—one is reminded of the scripture that says: "There is a way which *seemeth* right unto a man, but the end thereof are the ways of DEATH"(Proverbs 14:12).

While there is absolutely no reason to believe that the black clergy garments originated with Christ or the apostles, on the other hand, there is evidence of a Baalish priesthood that dressed in black garments! Our Lord said: "I will cut off the remnant of Baal from this place, and the name of the CHEMARIMS with the priests"(Zeph. 1:4). Now the "Chemarims" were the priests in BLACK garments (as has been noted by several Bible commentators), the word being taken from *chamar*, meaning "to be black." [1]

Since these ancient priests continually attended fires in which sacrifices were made, lighter colored clothes would have become more easily soiled by smoke. Perhaps for this reason, among the heathen priesthoods, black became associated with death and the practice of Black Garments became established. Though the original purpose of such garments has been almost entirely forgotten, it seems more than a mere coincidence that the priests of Modern Babylon are distinctly known to be wearers of BLACK!

And still another clue that will identify the Roman Catholic priesthood with the ancient priesthood may be seen in the use of the priestly *tonsure*. Now what is the tonsure? The tonsure is the shaving or clipping of a round spot on the head of priests at their ordination.[2] (See illustration.) The Council of Toledo in 633 A.D. made it a strict rule that all clerics must receive the circular tonsure of the crown of the head. And though the Catholic church attributes great importance to this rite, the practice is not Christian, but originated in heathenism!

Yes, the practice of shaving the head was a rite among pagan religions long before the Christian era. Gautama Buddha, who lived at least 540 years before our Lord's appearance on earth, shaved his head in obedience to a supposed divine command and caused others to follow his example. The priests of Bacchus, at their ordination, also received the tonsure. The priests of Osiris in Egypt were distinguished by the shaving of their heads. And in India, China, and Pagan Rome, the tonsure was also in evidence among the priesthoods that existed there.[3]

That the tonsure is an ancient custom, we also have the testimony of the Old Testament of our Bible! Our Lord, in direct ref-

1. Fausset, p. 291, Art.: "High Places."   3. Two Babylons, p. 221.
2. Encyclopedia of Religions, Vol. 3, p. 439.

erence to his ministers of that time, said: "They shall not make baldness upon their head" (Lev. 21:5). And that such "baldness" was the ROUNDED tonsure may be seen from Leviticus 19:27: "Ye shall not ROUND the corners of your heads." And so we see that not only is the use of the tonsure an ancient custom, but it is a practice that was directly and explicitly forbidden by God!

Now the reason the tonsure is forbidden is because it is of pagan significance. We will remember that in the Mysteries, many things had a hidden, a symbolic, meaning. And in the case of the tonsure, there was a paganistic meaning connected with the round shaving on the top of the head. It was nothing less than a Mystic image of the *sun* —a pagan symbol of the sun-god! The priests of Mithra "in their tonsure imitated the solar disk."[1] And this same practice, little by little, came to be used in the fallen church— Roman Catholicism. But in an attempt to discredit this fact, the councils of Valencia, Salzburg, and Ravenna associated the ROUND tonsure with the ROUND wafer that is served in the Catholic mass. However, there is nothing to indicate that the round wafer of the mass is a Christian symbol. In fact, the evidence is to the contrary. But more about this will have to wait until a section of the Chapter that follows.

1. Ibid, p. 222.

125

CHAPTER SEVENTEEN

The Mass

DO PRIESTS HAVE power to change the elements of bread and wine into the literal flesh and blood of Christ during the mass ritual? Is the Catholic belief in transubstantiation founded on the scriptures? Since Jesus at the Last Supper BROKE bread, why do Catholic priests serve an unbroken wafer? Why is it ROUND in shape? The Mystic letters I. H. S.—what do they mean? Was elaborate ritualism a part of the worship of the early church?

On the night that our Lord was betrayed, we read that "Jesus took bread, and blessed it, and brake it, and gave it to the disciples, and said, Take, eat; this is my body. And he took the cup and gave thanks, and gave it to them, saying, Drink ye all of it; For this is my blood of the New Testament, which is shed for many for the remission of sins"(Mt. 26:26-28). In this passage of scripture, Jesus used the expression "this IS my body" in reference to the bread; and in referring to the wine, he said, "this IS my blood." The Roman Catholic church insists that when the wine and wafer is consecrated by a priest, it becomes the *actual* flesh and the *actual* blood of Christ! This is known as transubstantiation. But does a piece of bread or a cup of wine really become the flesh and blood of Christ? Is this what our Lord meant?

To those who study *all* that the Bible says on the subject, it becomes evident that our Lord's reference to his body and blood was SYMBOLIC. He simply meant that these elements represented or were symbols of his flesh and blood. We know that these elements did not become the literal flesh and blood of Jesus when he "blessed" them, because HE (literally) was still there! He was sitting there with them before, during, and after they partook of the bread and cup. He was not changed from a *person* into some liquid and bread! His flesh was still on his bones and his blood still in his veins—he, as a person, had not vanished away to reappear in the form of a piece of bread or a cup of wine! No, when Jesus spoke of the bread and wine as his body and blood, he was using symbolic language. Such symbolism is often found in the Bible.

One time three of David's friends heard him express a strong desire for water from the well at Bethlehem. In spite of extreme danger, these men broke through the host of the Philistines and brought the water to him. When David found out that these men had risked their lives in this way, he refused to drink the water, saying: "Is not this the blood of the men who went in jeopardy of their lives?"(2 Sam. 23:17). No one would suppose that David meant this water was literal blood. No, he used the expression in a *figurative* sense.

Likewise, the Bible gives references to eating flesh, drinking blood, eating a book, hungering after righteousness, etc. —all of which are shown by the context to be figurative expressions. Jesus once said, "I am the door"(John 10:9). Surely no one would suppose that Jesus was or became a literal door! Could we point at a door and say, "This is Jesus"? Obviously such an expression is figurative. On another occasion, our Lord said, "I am the vine, ye are the branches"(John 15:5). Certainly he did not mean that he had become a literal vine! The scriptures speak of our Lord as a rock, "and that rock was Christ"(1 Cor. 10:4). But certainly he is not a literal rock. It would be rank heathenism for us to set up a rock and say, "This is God." No, these references to our Lord as a rock, vine, and door, are figurative— symbolical. And when Jesus said, "This is my body...This is my blood", it was also figurative.

But for centuries, Romanism has insisted on a LITERAL inter-pretation of our Lord's words on this point. They believe that after the bread and wine are consecrated by a priest, the wine is no longer wine and the bread is no longer bread. But our Lord, even AFTER he had blessed the sacrament, still called it "the fruit of the vine" —not his literal blood. (See Matt. 26:29). If the elements of the communion become the actual flesh and blood of Christ, how could we take it "in *remembrance*...until he comes" if he thus becomes present in body, blood, soul, and diety? If the wine becomes literal blood during the mass ritual—as is claimed—then to drink it would be forbidden by the scriptures. (Acts 15:20, etc.)

Perhaps the most obvious proof that the Catholic theory of transubstantiation is a fraud, however, is the simple fact that there is absolutely no change in the elements after they are suppos-edly changed into flesh and blood! Now of necessity, Romanism acknowledges that there is no VISIBLE change to the communion elements. They have the same taste, color, smell, weight, and dimensions, after they are supposedly changed into the body and blood of Christ. The bread still looks like bread, tastes like bread, smells like bread, and feels like bread. But in the Catholic mind it is not bread, it is the flesh of God. And the wine: It still looks like wine, tastes like wine, smells like wine, and if you drink enough of it, it would make you drunk like wine. But the devout Catholic must believe that it is blood, God-blood. The whole idea is one great contradiction.

In spite of this, Catholics are strictly required to believe that the elements are really changed into the flesh and blood of Christ. If they do not accept this dogma, they are told that they will be eternally lost; that the belief in transubstantiation is essential to salvation! Thus spake the learned Council of Trent when it officially defined the doctrine of transubstantiation and pronounced curses upon anyone who would deny it.

The poem on page 141 is not included for the sake of being unkind, but to illustrate the inconsistency of the teaching that priests have power to change bread and wine into the flesh and blood of Christ. (See poem).

When the priest supposedly changes the bread and wine into flesh and blood, he says the Latin words: "Hoc est corpus meus." In view of the fact that no change is made, we can understand how the expression "HOCUS-POCUS" originated with these words![1]

The Catechism of the Council of Trent required pastors to explain that not only did the elements of the mass contain flesh, bones, and nerves as a *part* of Christ, "but also a WHOLE CHRIST."[2] Then, when the priest offers it up, he is believed to be actually sacrificing Christ AGAIN! Thus it is referred to as the "SACRIFICE of the Mass" and as "a *renewal* of the sacrifice of the cross."[3] The catechism books teach that the reason that the mass is the same sacrifice as that of Calvary is because the victim in each case is Jesus Christ.[4] Such a belief, of course, was the natural outcome of the doctrine that the elements of the communion became literally a "Christ." This led to another grievous and unscriptural error: Instead of Calvary being a *finished* work, once for all, the Catholic church had to teach that each mass is a continuation of the same sacrifice!

This presented quite a theological problem. If each sacrifice of the mass is a new sacrifice of Christ, then instead of Christ being offered ONCE, he has instead been offered MILLIONS of times through the centuries since his death at Calvary! But do the

1. The Story of Civilization, p. 749.   3. A Catholic Word List, p. 45.   931.
2. Encyclopedia of Religions, Vol. 2, p. 77.   4. The New Baltimore Catechism, No. 3, Question

scriptures teach that the sacrifice of Calvary was to be continually repeated? Or was it a *completed* work, once for all time?

Let us notice the scriptural testimony. In Hebrews 9:25-28, we find a comparison of the ONE sacrifice of Christ with those numerous sacrifices of the Old Testament: Our Lord did not need to offer himself often (as the priests had to continually make sacrifices) but "ONCE" hath he appeared to put away sin by the sacrifice of himself; "And as it is appointed unto men ONCE to die... SO Christ was ONCE offered to bear the sins of many; and unto them that look for him shall he appear the second time without sin unto salvation." Certainly there is no hint of the doctrine that Christ was to be offered millions of time! No, ONCE for all the Supreme Sacrifice was made.

In the Old Testament, sacrifices had to be continually offered because none of them was the PERFECT sacrifice. But when the perfect sacrifice was made—the sacrifice of our Lord himself—there was no longer any need for repeated sacrifices. Thus "we are sanctified through the offering of the body of Jesus Christ ONCE for all. For every priest standeth daily ministering and offering oftentimes the same sacrifices, which can never take away sins: But this man (Christ), after he had offered ONE sacrifice for sins for ever, sat down on the right hand of God...for by ONE offering he perfected forever them that are sanctified." (Heb. 10:10-14). Notice the striking contrast here! The priests of the Old Testament had to "stand" to offer sacrifices. Why? Because their sacrifice was not the final one, not the *perfect* one. But when Christ presented his sacrifice, he "sat down." Why? Because his was the final, the perfect, the once-for-all sacrifice.

There is not ONE verse in the Bible that even *hints* at the idea that the sacrifice of Christ has to be continued. The scriptures, to the contrary, continually stress just the opposite. The combined testimony of the Bible is that Christ was the perfect sacrifice; that he gave himself ONCE; and that this sacrifice settled the sin problem FOREVER. Christ will not need to come and be offered again. Yet Catholics are taught that he has been offered on their altars millions of times since he cried, "It is finished." They believe that each mass is a fresh sacrifice of Christ. To such a teaching this scripture could apply: "Seeing they crucify to themselves the Son of God afresh, and put him to an open shame"(Heb. 6:6). And this they do about 100,000 times a day throughout the world in the ritual of the Mass!

Now after the bread has supposedly been changed into a "Christ" by the priest, it is placed on a monstrance. A *monstrance* is

129

made in the shape of a cross with a hollow center in which the "consecrated" piece of bread is placed. This is surrounded by a SUNBURST design.[1] Before this monstrance the Catholic must bow and worship the little wafer as GOD! Such a practice is rank idolatry and is very similar to the practices of pagan tribes who worship fetishes. Such false ritualism and worship is one of the great errors to which the transubstantiation doctrine led.

Adopting the idea that the elements of the Lord's supper become the literal flesh and blood of Christ presented other problems. Tertullian tells us that priests took great care that no crumb should fall—lest the body of Jesus be hurt! In the middle ages, there were serious discussions as to what should be done if a person were to vomit after receiving the sacrament or if a dog or mouse were by chance to eat God's body. At the Council of Constance, it was argued that if a communicant spilled some of the blood on his beard, both beard and the man with the beard should be destroyed by burning![2]

By the end of the Eleventh Century, lest someone should spill God's blood, the Catholic church began to hold back the cup from the people. (But was it not also possible that the early disciples could have spilled some of the cup? Our Lord did not withold it from them on such a basis!) Finally, in 1415, the Council of Constance officially denied the cup to laymen. And to this day, members of Catholic congregations do not drink of the cup. Only the priest is permitted to do this. Catholics are told that they do not need to drink the cup, because the blood is contained in the flesh. Why then does the priest drink the wine? Why not just eat the flesh? And if the priest can drink the wine on behalf of the whole assembly, then why couldn't he also eat the bread for them?

Obviously, the idea of the congregation taking only *part* of what Jesus instructed us to take, is contrary to the Bible. Such a perversion of the plain instructions of God's Word must come from that great deceiver, the Devil. And a church that forms such doctrines cannot be that Church spoken of in the Bible as pure and undefiled.

All of these errors we have mentioned were the result of adopting the doctrines of transubstantiation, the idea that the elements

1. Handbook of Catholic Practices, p.20.
2. The Other Side of Rome, p.21.

130

of bread and wine become the actual flesh and blood of Christ. But why and how did this doctrine enter the Catholic church? It seems apparent that the adopting of transubstantiation into the Romish church was but another compromise that was made with paganism, for pagan religions held ideas that were very similar to the transubstantiation theory. In the noted work "Hasting's Encyclopedia of Religion and Ethics", are many pages devoted to an article entitled "Eating the god." In these pages, abundant evidence is given of transubstantiation rites among many nations, tribes, and religions.

The historian Durant tells us that the belief in transubstantiation as practiced in the Roman Catholic church is "one of the oldest ceremonies of *primitive* religion."[1] A type of Eucharist was celebrated in Egypt, for example, in which a mest cake was consecrated by a priest and was suppose to become the flesh of Osiris. This was then eaten and wine was taken as a part of the rite.[2]

The cakes and *Haoma* drink of Mithra, as well as the idea of transubstantiation, were a part of the religion of Mithraism and were similar to the Catholic Eucharist today.[3] And that such ideas were believed in Pagan Rome is certain from Cicero's rhetorical question about the corn of Ceres and the wine of Bacchus.

Even in Mexico and Central America, among those who had never heard of Christ, was the belief in eating the flesh of their deity. When the Roman Catholic missionaries first landed in Mexico and Central America, "their surprise was heightened, when they witnessed a religious rite which reminded them of communion ...an image made of flour... and after consecration by priests, was distributed among the people who ate it... declaring it was the flesh of the deity... "[4](note)

In one form or another then, the idea of eating the flesh of the god spread to many nations and tribes. When Rome conquered the world, it absorbed many of these rites into its religious system. Later, when Christianity swept into the Empire, many noticed there were some points of similarity between the rites of the pagans and those of the Christians. Eventually the two systems were merged together. Church leaders of the fallen church disguised the pagan rites with Christian sounding names and this deceptive mixture has deceived the world! In order to induce both pagans and those who had believed in Christ into her arms, the

1. The Story of Civilization, p. 741.
2. Encyclopedia of Religions, Vol. 2, p. 76.
(Note: Actually, the idea of eating the flesh of a god was of CANNIBALISTIC inception! Heathen priests, it is known, ate a portion of all sacrifices that were made as a part of their ritual. Some of these sacrifices were HUMAN sacrifices! Thus, the priests of Nimrod or Baal were

3. Ibid.
4. Prescott's Mexico, vol. 3.

required to eat human flesh. These priests were known as "Cahna-Bal", that is, "the priest of Baal." And it is from this expression that we derive our modern word "cannibal"—a devourer of human flesh! —Hislop, p. 232.)

131

fallen church had to adopt the idea of eating and drinking the literal flesh and literal blood of their god! And thus, transubstantiation—a *pagan* doctrine—entered the professing church.

But besides this clue as to how pagan rites were mixed into the "church", there is also much other evidence just beneath the surface. During the Catholic Mass, those members of the Romish church who are in good standing, come forward and kneel before the priest who places a piece of bread in their mouth — which they believe has become a "Christ." The accompanying illustration shows the way this is pictured in the Catholic catechism books.[1]

Now this piece of bread that is served is called a host.[2] Its shape "must" be ROUND.[3] (The illustration shows the way the "host" is pictured in a Catholic picture dictionary.) But in the memorial supper instituted by our Lord, he took bread and *broke* it. Certainly unleavened bread does not break into ROUND pieces! The scriptures explain that the *breaking* of the bread represents our Lord's body which was broken for us by the cruel beatings and stripes. But in the Catholic Mass, the bread is NOT BROKEN. The round, disk shapped wafer is served completely whole, and thus do they spoil the import of the figure which Jesus gave to represent his broken body!

Seeing then that the use of the *round* wafer is contrary to the scriptures, we can logically ask why it came to be used in the Catholic Church. Here again, another compromise with paganism is apparent! We know this, because the round wafer is nothing more nor less than an ancient symbol of the *sun!* "The 'round' wafer, whose 'roundness' is so important an element in the Romish Mystery," says Hislop, "is only another symbol of Baal, or the sun."[4]

Such round cakes were used in the ancient Mysteries in Egypt. In writing of these rites, Wilkinson says: "The thin, round cake occurs on all altars" of Egypt.[5] When the Mysteries came to Rome under the name of Mithraism, the higher initiates of the

1. The Official Revised Baltimore Catechism, p. 131.   4. Two Babylons, p. 163.
2. A Latin word meaning victim or sacrifice.   5. Egyptians, Vol. 5, p. 353.
3. The Handbook of Catholic Practices, p. 231.

system received a small round cake or wafer of unleavened bread which symbolized the solar disk.[1] And so we see to what a great extent the Romish church adopted paganism, laying aside the scriptural ordinance of the BROKEN bread, substituting rather the round sun-symbol wafer of paganism!

In 1854 an ancient temple was discovered in Egypt with inscriptions that show these little round cakes on an altar. Above the altar is a large image of the sun.[2] A similar sun-symbol was used above the altar of a temple near the town of Babain, in upper Egypt, where there is a representation of the sun, before which two priests are shown worshipping. (See drawing.)

But this use of the *sun image* above the "altar" was not limited to Egypt. Even in far away Peru, South America, this same image was known and worshipped.[3] Now if there be any doubt in the reader's mind that the round host of the Catholic mass descended from ancient sun-worship and is indeed a sun-symbol, he may simply compare the sun image before which the heathen bowed with the monstrance sun-image —in the center of which the host is placed as a "sun" and before which the Roman Catholic bows today—and he will immediately see the striking similarity! (See page 130).

Even among the Israelites of the Old Testament, when they departed from the Lord and worshipped Baal, they too set up sun-images above their altars! But during the reign of Josiah, these images were torn down: "And they brake down the altars of Baalim in his presence; and the images (Margin, SUN-images) that were ON HIGH above them..."(2 Chron. 34:4). The displeasure of our God against such sun-images, even though they were used by his own people, is apparent!

Yet—and this sounds shocking—the very same type of sun-

1. Isis Unveiled, p. 351.
2. Ancient Pagan and Modern Christian Symbolism, p. 34.
3. Story of the World's Worship, p. 383.

images that pagans used, are found above the "altar" in the "Mother" church of Catholicism, St. Peter's Cathedral at Rome. As the photo on the next page shows, in the very middle of the cross-shapped Cathedral[1] is a huge canopy—95 feet high —which is supported by four pillars, twisted in serpent-like form, slightly covered by branches. Near the top of these pillars—"on high above" the most important altar in Catholicism—are sun-images in exactly the same form as the ones used by the pagans in ancient times! (See photo.)

Then high on the back wall of St. Peter's, as the photo also shows, is another sun-image. This one is a huge and elaborate golden sun-burst, which from the front of the church, also appears "above" the main altar of the Cathedral. And it is evident that such is Babylonish, for the Great Temple of Babylon also exhibited the golden sun-image for the worship of the ancient people.[2]

The circular sun-image design at the back of a church—above the altar—has been repeatedly used in thousands of churches and Cathedrals to this very day, as seen in the accompanying illustration of a church in Italy. This same type of window or design has also been placed above the *doorways* of hundreds of church buildings throughout the world. But this again, like the other uses of the sun-symbol, is but a continuation of ancient pagan symbolism! Not only do many church buildings feature this symbol above their entrances, but so did the ancient temples of Babylon and Egypt! In Babylon, there were temples with images of the sun-god to face the rising sun which were placed above the entry![3] An early Babylonian Temple built by King Gudea, for example, featured such an emblem of the sun-god over the entrance.[4] Borrowing this usage from the Babylonians, it became a custom for Egyptian builders to place a solar disk (sometimes with wings, or other emblems) over the entrance to their temples—to honour the sun-god and drive away evil spirits.[5]

Another symbol of the sun was a round circle with crossing lines which resembled a spoked wheel—the wheel of a CHARIOT.

1. See page 43(c).   3. Architecture, Nature, and Magic, p. 29.
2. Hislop, p. 162.   4. Ibid, p. 112.

The ancients thought of the sun as a great chariot driven by the sun-god who made his trip across the heavens each day, and passed through the underworld at night. And so the symbol of the sun chariot—its wheel—came to be associated with sunworship. Even when God's own people mixed Baal religion into their worship, they had "chariots of the sun"—chariots dedicated to the sun-god! (2 Kings 23:4-11). But getting back to the chariot sun-symbol, the wheel, it is interesting to notice that this Babylonish symbol has repeatedly been used by the fallen church of Rome. This wheel-sun-symbol is placed over the famous statue of "Peter" in St. Peter's Cathedral.

A tablet found in the land of Babylon (and now in a British Museum) shows one of the Babylonian kings restoring a symbol of the sun-god in the temple of Bel. This sun-symbol is an eight pointed cross, similar to a wheel. And it is this same eight-point-cross-wheel design that marks the pavement of the circular square before St. Peter's church! (See pages 41 and 43.)

Surrounding the high altar of St. Peter's (beneath which Catholics are taught that Peter is buried) there are also numerous sun-images in the design of the floor! (Notice closely photo on Page 135). The Romish pictures of Mary and the saints always feature the circular sun-symbol disk around their heads! Catholic priests receive the round tonsure on their heads, even as the priestly sun-worshippers of olden times. The round sun images are seen above the altars of many Roman Catholic Cathedrals and over their entrances—in much the same way as they were used among pagans. The monstrance in which the round host is placed features a sun-burst design. All of these uses of sun-symbols may seem insignificant at first glance, but when the *over all* picture is seen, each of them is a clue to help us solve the Mystery about Babylon in our times.

And it is this same sun-symbolism that is carried out in the use of the round host of the Catholic communion ritual. One of the ways that Catholic catechism books picture the Mass is with a drawing of these round wafers marked with a cross: ⊕⊕⊕[1] We can't help but notice how similar this is in appearance to the round wafers seen on the Assyrian monument drawing which we have reproduced on the next page. In this scene, one man is bowing before a Priest-king and below a sun-image. The second

1. Baltimore Catechism.

136

man from the right is bringing forth an offering of round wafers marked with a cross! It seems evident then that simply because a cross is placed on the round Catholic hosts does not "Christianize" them, for the cross was a religious symbol among many religions—long before the Christian era. And there is evidence that the round sacred cakes of the Mysteries in Egypt were marked with this very symbol also! [1]

But now to look again at the round host, we notice that the Mystic letters I. H. S. are written on it. A study of these letters provides us with another identification mark— another clue in the mystery—that shows further pagan influence in the Roman Catholic mass. Many suppose that these letters are of Christian origin, for indeed they are used in various ways in both Catholic and Protestant churches. We are told that these letters I. H. S. mean "Iesus Hominum Salvator"; that is, "Jesus the Saviour of Men"; or, "In Hoc Signo", the words Constantine claimed to see in his cross vision.

It is very possible, however, that these letters could be taken two ways. If so, their use was only another compromise that Rome made with paganism. You see, during the days of the Emperors, there were many worshippers of Isis (the Egyptian form of the Babylonian Goddess) at Rome. Let one of them cast his eyes upon the letters. What did these letters mean to him? To the worshipper of the Goddess, these letters said: "Isis, Horus, Seb", or in other words, "The Mother, the Child, and the Father of the gods"— the Egyptian Trinity. [2]

These letters are definitely of a pre-Christian origin, for they were used in the monogram of the pagan god Bacchus; they also appeared on the coins of the Maharajah of Cashmere. [3]

Now when our Lord instituted the memorial supper of the bread and the cup, it was at NIGHT. He did not take it at breakfast time, or at lunch time. It was at night. And likewise, the original

1. Bonwick's Egyptian Belief, p. 148; Pentateuch Examined, vol. 6, p. 115. 2. Two Babylons, p. 164.
3. Bible Myths, p. 351.

Christians partook of the Lord's supper at night, following the example set by Christ himself and the types of the Old Testament. But as the days of the departure from the original pattern came, the Lord's supper came to be observed at a *morning* meeting.[1]

But how and why did this change come about? As we have seen, one of the leading branches of the "Mysteries" at Rome was known as Mithraism. This religion practiced certain rites which—in some ways—resembled the communion of the Christians. However, the Mithraic rites were observed early in the morning—the idea being associated with the sun, with dawn—the rising of their sun god. When the falling away came, as we have seen, great compromises were made by church leaders in an attempt to merge the two sides into one apostate religion. And such a merger is evidenced in the transfer of the Lord's supper from its observance at NIGHT to early morning—to make the rites of the two opposing religions appear to be more similar. Roman Catholic churches still have their early mass in which the communion elements are taken. And when the Protestant Reformation came, they too followed this practice of taking the Lord's "supper" in the morning, only not quite as early in the morning as the Roman Church!

Another doctrine that was borrowed from paganism (which also encouraged the transfer of the communion supper from night to early morning) was the belief that the partaker must be *fasting* before taking communion. Obviously early morning would be an easier time to meet this fasting requirement than at night. However, the idea that a person must be fasting before receiving communion is very inconsistent and contrary to the Bible. In fact, it was after our Lord had just *eaten* that he instituted the memorial supper! (Matt. 26:20-26).

While there is no indication in the Holy Scriptures that a person must be fasting before receiving communion, there was such a requirement that was a part of the Mystery religion. Those who sought initiation in the Elusinian Mysteries were first asked: "Are you fasting?" If their answer was no, initiation was denied.[2]

Now of course the Bible does teach fasting and prayer. But *true* fasting must come from the heart. When and how long to fast may differ with the individual and is dependent upon the purpose for which the fasting is done. However, for a mortal man to dictate when a person must fast is condemned in the scriptures. Such is only a mere form or rule, not a heart-felt conviction. And of such fasting, God says: "When they fast, I will not hear their cry" (Jer. 14:12). The Pharisees were strict about fasting on cer-

1. The Growth of the Christian Church, p. 23.
2. Two Babylons, p. 164.

138

tain days, but neglected the weightier matters of the law (Mt. 6:16). And the apostle Paul warned about man-made commandments to "abstain from meats" as being a mark of apostasy (1 Tim. 4:3).

Finally, in addition to the proof that has been given, the mass ritual is seen to be paganistic by the elaborate ceremony and magnificence it features. In commenting on the mass ceremony, "Romanism and the Gospel" says: "It is a spectacle of gorgeous magnificence—lights, colours, vestments, music, incense, and what has a strange psychological effect, a number of drilled officiants performing a stately ritual in entire independence of the worshippers. These are indeed spectators, not participants, spectators like those who were present at a performance of the ancient MYSTERY CULTS."[1]

A noted work on Roman Catholicism, summarizes the mechanical performance made by the priest during mass in these words: "He makes the sign of the cross sixteen times; turns toward the congregation six times; lifts his eyes to heaven eleven times; kisses the altar eight times; folds his hands four times; strikes his breast ten times, bows his head twenty-one times; genuflects eight times; bows his shoulders seven times; blesses the altar with the sign of the cross thirty times; lays his hands flat on the altar twenty-nine times; prays secretly eleven times; prays aloud thirteen times; takes the bread and wine and turns it into the body and blood of Christ (?); covers and uncovers the chalice ten times; goes to and fro twenty times; and in addition performs numerous other acts."[2] Adding to this complicated ritualism is the use of highly coloured robes, candles, bells, incense, music, mournful singing in Latin, and the showy pageantry for which the Roman church is known. What a contrast this is to the *simple* memorial supper instituted by our Lord! In that supper, Jesus simply took bread, gave thanks, broke it and gave it to his disciples. In like manner also, he took the cup and from it they drank. No elaborate ritualism! No forms and ceremonies! No air of mysterious display!

But not being content with the simple, sincere, memorial supper of Christ, the Roman Church attempted to compete with the elaborate rituals of paganism. This was how and why ritualism came to be mixed with the Lord's supper—and this mixture produced the Romish ceremony known as the Mass. But adopting such ritualism is a sure indication of how far the fallen church had fallen! You see, the ritualistic rites of the pagans were in honour of pagan gods or demons! And that Paul was aware of these counterfeit rites is evidenced in his writings to the Corinthians: "The cup

1. p. 93.
2. Roman Catholicism, p. 170.

of blessing which we bless", he wrote, "is it not the communion of the blood of Christ? The bread which we break, is it not the communion of the body of Christ?...But I say, that the things which the Gentiles sacrifice, they sacrifice to devils, and not to God: and I would not that ye should have fellowship with devils. Ye cannot drink the cup of the Lord, and the CUP OF DEVILS: ye cannot be partakers of the Lord's table, and the TABLE OF DEVILS" (1 Cor. 10:16-21). In the next chapter, Paul gave instructions to the Corinthian church for the proper observance of the Lord's supper. Possibly, even at that early date, there was a tendency among those that lived in Corinth—a pagan stronghold—to mix the true Lord's supper with that counterfeit ritual of the pagans.

The following table shows a comparison between the communion supper instituted by Christ and that of the Catholic mass today:

THE LORD'S SUPPER	ROMAN CATHOLIC MASS
The bread was broken.	The bread is served whole, round.
Was taken at night.	Taken early in the morning.
Taken after eating a meal.	Partaker must be fasting.
Instituted by Jesus.	A mixture with paganism.
Bread and cup represents the Lord's body and blood.	Bread and wine are said to become flesh and blood.
Both the bread and the fruit of the vine were taken.	Only the bread may be eaten by the congregation.
Representative of a finished work—of a perfect sacrifice.	Each mass is suppose to be a fresh sacrifice of Christ.
A simple blessing was given over the elements.	Long prayers are chanted for the living and dead.
Featured the simplicity of a common meal.	Elaborate ritualism, rites.

A ROMAN MIRACLE (?)

A pretty maid, a Protestant, was to a Catholic wed;
To love all Bible truths and tales, quite early she'd been bred.
  It sorely grieved her husband's heart that she would not comply
And join the Mother Church of Rome and heretics deny.

So day by day he flattered her, but still she saw no good
Would ever come from bowing down to idols made of wood;
  The mass, the host, the miracles, were made but to deceive;
And transubstantiation, too, she'd never dare believe.

He went to see his clergyman and told him his sad tale
"My wife's an unbeliever, sir, you can perhaps, prevail;
  For all your Romish miracles my wife has strong aversion,
To really work a miracle may lead to her conversion."

The priest went with the gentleman—he thought to gain a prize.
He said, "I will convert her, sir, and open both her eyes."
  So when they came into the house, the husband loudly cried,
"The priest has come to dine with us!" "He's welcome," she replied.

And when, at last, the meal was o'er, the priest at once began
To teach his hostess all about the sinful state of man;
  The greatness of our Saviour's love, which Christians can't deny
To give Himself a sacrifice and for our sins to die.

"I will return tomorrow, lass, prepare some bread and wine;
The sacramental miracle will stop your soul's decline."
  "I'll bake the bread," the lady said. "You may," he did reply,
"And when you've seen this miracle, convinced you'll be, say I."

The priest did come accordingly, the bread and wine did bless.
The lady asked, "Sir, is it changed?" The priest answered, "Yes,
  It's changed from common bread and wine to truly flesh and blood;
Begorra, lass, this power of mine has changed it into God!"

So having blessed the bread and wine, to eat they did prepare;
The lady said unto the priest, "I warn you to take care,
  For half an ounce of arsenic was mixed right in the batter,
But since you have its nature changed, it cannot really matter."

The priest was struck real dumb—he looked as pale as death.
The bread and wine fell from his hands and he did gasp for breath.
  "Bring me my horse!" the priest cried, "This is a cursed home!"
The lady replied, "Begone; tis you who shares the curse of Rome."

The husband, too, he sat surprised, and not a word did say.
At length he spoke, "My dear," said he, "The priest has run away;
  To gulp such mummery and tripe, I'm not, for sure, quite able;
I'll go with you and will renounce this Roman Catholic Fable."

Author Unknown

CHAPTER EIGHTEEN

Three Days and Nights

MOST OF US have assumed that Jesus died on "Good Friday" and rose from the dead early on "Easter" Sunday morning. Since Jesus said he would rise "the third day", some count part of Friday as one day, Saturday as the second, and part of Sunday as the third. But when we take a closer look at the scriptures, we find that Jesus spoke of the time period between his burial and resurrection as three days AND three nights. From Friday afternoon until Sunday morning is not three days and three nights! What then is the correct explanation?

When the Pharisees came to Jesus asking for a sign that he was truly the Messiah, he told them that no sign would be given them, except the sign of the prophet Jonas. "For as Jonas was THREE DAYS AND THREE NIGHTS in the whale's belly," he answered, "so shall the son of man be THREE DAYS AND THREE NIGHTS in the heart of the earth" (Mt. 12:38-40; Jonah 1:17).

In other verses, Jesus said he would rise "the third day"(Mt. 16:21; Mk. 10:34; Lk. 24:7). There is no contradiction—as some have supposed—between this expression and the term "three days and three nights." Both expressions are used interchangeably in the scriptures. Turning to Genesis, for example, we read that "God divided the light from the darkness. And God called the light day, and the darkness he called night. And the evening (darkness) and the morning (light) were the FIRST DAY...and the evening (darkness) and the morning (light) were the SECOND DAY...and the evening (now three periods of night) and the morning (now three periods of light) were THE THIRD DAY" (Gen. 1:4-13). Here then is an example of the term "the third day" counted up and shown to include three days AND three nights.

Bearing in mind that Jesus rose "the third day", let us notice that Sunday is not the third day after Friday: One day after Friday is Saturday, the second day after Friday is Sunday, and THE THIRD DAY after Friday is Monday! Mark 8:31 says that Jesus would "be killed and AFTER three days rise again." Let us count these days. If Jesus was killed on Friday, and then after one day the resurrection took place, it would have been on Saturday; after two days would have been Sunday; and after three days, it would have been on Monday. It seems evident then that there is something wrong with the wide-spread belief about Friday as the day of the crucifixion or Sunday as the day of the resurrection—*or both!*

Since there are twelve hours in a day and twelve hours in a night (John 11:9,10), "three days and three nights" would equal 72 hours as the time element between our Lord's burial and his resurrection. But was this time element EXACTLY 72 hours?

According to the scriptures, Jesus was in the tomb NO LESS than 72 hours. He was in the tomb for "three days and three nights" and he arose "after three days"(Mt. 12:40; Mk. 8:31). We see no reason to figure this at any less than a full 72 hours. On the other hand, according to the scriptures, Jesus was in the tomb NO LONGER than 72 hours. Jesus said, "Destroy this temple, and IN three days I will raise it up...he spake of the temple of his body." The time element here expressed could not be any more than 72 hours, for if it was, then Jesus would not have risen IN the third day. In fact, even one minute more than 72 hours would have been in the FOURTH day, since 72 hours is the full total of time in three complete days and nights!

Therefore, since the scriptures indicate that Jesus was in the tomb no less than 72 hours and no more than 72 hours, it seems definitely implied that the time element was exactly 72 hours. If this is true, it is certainly not out of line with the fact that God is a God of EXACTNESS. He does everything right on schedule. Nothing is accidental with him.

It was "when the fulness of the time was come"—not one year too early, or one year too late, but right on time—"God sent forth his Son"(Gal. 4:4). The time when he was to be anointed was foreordained and was spoken of by the prophet Daniel, as was also the time when Jesus would be "cut off" for the sins of the people. Those who tried to kill him before this failed, for "his time was not yet come"! And not only was the year and time of his death foreordained, but even the very HOUR was a part of the Divine plan! "Father", Jesus prayed, "the HOUR is come..."(John 17:1).

Now since there was an exact time for Christ to be born, an exact time for his anointing, an exact time for his ministry to begin, and an exact time for his death, it should not be regarded as inconsistent to believe that there was also an exact time period that was to elapse between his burial and resurrection—72 hours exactly.

143

Bearing this in mind, we can now understand what *time of day* that the resurrection took place! Since Jesus was in the tomb three days and three nights (72 hours), we know that the resurrection took place at the same time of day that he was buried—only three days later. In other words, if he was buried at dawn, then he would rise exactly at dawn—three days later. Or if he was buried at noon, then his resurrection would take place at noon. If he was buried in the evening, then his resurrection would take place in the evening—three days later. If we can find out what time of day that Jesus was buried, we will automatically know what time of day he rose!

The Bible tells us that Jesus died shortly after "the ninth hour" or three in the afternoon.[1] (Matt. 27:46-50; Mk. 15:34-37; Lk. 23:44 -46). According to the reckoning of time in the Bible, each day ended and a new day began at sundown (Lev. 23:32). And since our Lord was crucified on the "preparation", the day before the "high day" sabbath, special measures were taken to be sure that his body was removed before sundown—before the high day sabbath began: "The Jews therefore, because it was the preparation, that the bodies should not remain upon the cross on the sabbath day, for that sabbath was an HIGH DAY,) besought Pilate that their legs might be broken, and that they might be taken away... but when they came to Jesus... he was dead already"(John 19:31-33). He was then taken down from the cross and buried in the tomb of Joseph of Arimathaea "for the sepulchre was night at hand" (John 19:42). These things took place "when the even was come"—the Greek word here translated "even" is *"opsios,"* meaning in the "late afternoon"(Mk. 15:42).

Therefore, since the resurrection of Jesus was to take place three days later, but at the same time of day as when he was buried, we know what time of day he arose! He was buried in the late afternoon, so of course his resurrection took place in the late afternoon—three days later. We know for certain that the resurrection did not take place at sunrise—as is sometimes assumed—for Jesus wasn't buried at sunrise! This is also evident from the fact that when visitors came to the tomb as the next day was dawning, the tomb was already empty (Mk. 16:2). Nor did Jesus rise during the night, for he was not buried during the night! He was in the tomb three days and three nights, but he rose the third DAY—not at night!

1. Daylight hours in the Bible are divided into four divisions, beginning at sunrise and ending at sun down. The third hour would be 9 AM, the sixth hour 12 noon, the ninth hour 3 PM, and the twelveth hour 6 PM.

On what day then was the resurrection? The Bible tells us that when Mary Magdalene came to the tomb early on the first day of the week, "it was yet DARK", and Jesus was NOT there (John 20: 1,2). The gospel writers tell of several different visits made by the disciples to the tomb on that Sunday morning. In EVERY instance, they found the tomb EMPTY! An angel said: "He is not here: for he is risen, as he said" (Mt. 28:6).

Therefore, since the scriptures indicate that Jesus rose before sundown, and since he was not in the tomb early Sunday morning, we can conclude that the resurrection took place late in the afternoon of the day before. According to this, the resurrection was late on Saturday afternoon.

But doesn't the Bible somewhere say that Christ rose on the first day of the week—very early in the morning? The Bible tells us that the first day of the week was when the disciples *discovered* that he was risen—Mt. 28:1-6; Mk. 16:2-6; Lk. 24:1,2; John 20:1,2 —but not one of these verses teaches that this was the time of the resurrection! In each instance the tomb was empty! He was already risen!

Some have thought, however, that Mark 16:9 teaches that the resurrection was early Sunday morning. Here is the verse: "Now when Jesus was risen early the first day of the week, he appeared first to Mary Magdalene, out of whom he had cast seven devils." But this verse does not say that Jesus rose on the first day of the week. Look at it closely. Does it say that early on the first day of the week that Jesus was "rising" or that he "did rise" at that time? No! It says that when the first day of the week came, he "WAS RISEN." This is the past perfect tense; that is, he was already risen.

The Greek word here rendered "was risen" is *"anastas"* and has the meaning of "having risen", indefinitely in the PAST. Neither the Greek or English wording of this verse indicates that Christ rose early in the morning of the first day of the week. Instead, he was already risen.

A study of Mark 16:9 (note) and the following verses through verse 14, shows that Mark is telling of the various *appearances*

Note: When the Bible was originally written, commas (and other punctuation marks) were completely unknown. Punctuation marks were invented by Aldus Manutious in the Fifteenth Century. Since the original manuscripts had no punctuation marks, the translators placed commas wherever they thought they should go —based entirely on their beliefs. In Mark 16: 9, notice where the comma is placed: "Now when Jesus was risen early the first day of the week, he appeared first to Mary Magdalene." Placing the comma here seems to connect the first day of the week with the time of the resurection. But, if the comma had been placed after risen, it would read like this: "Now when Jesus was risen, early the first day of the week he appeared first to Mary Magdalene..." Is the scripture explaining the time of the resurection OR the time when Jesus appeared to Mary? The context, other verses, the fact

that Jesus made on the first day of the week. The context makes it clear that he is not explaining which day the resurrection took place.

When Sunday morning came, our Lord was already RISEN, having risen late in the afternoon of the day before. On which day then was the crucifixion? Since we believe that Jesus did fulfill his sign, we can count back three days which brings us to Wednesday as the day of the crucifixion. Would this make three days and three nights between the burial and resurrection of Christ? Yes. Let us count the days and nights and see. Wednesday night, Thursday night, and Friday night—three nights; also Thursday, Friday, and Saturday—three days. This would make a total of exactly three days and three nights or 72 hours.

One day after Wednesday would be Thursday. Two days after Wednesday would be Friday, and "the third day" after Wednesday would be Saturday. Here then is perfect scriptural harmony! Jesus was buried on Wednesday just before sundown; he rose Saturday just before sundown. Truly he fulfilled his sign of three days and three nights, rising the third day.

Some have been confused about Luke 24:21, which records the words of the two disciples on the road to Emmaus: "But we trusted that it had been he which should have redeemed Israel", they said, "and beside all this, to day is the THIRD day since these things were done." Now because Jesus appeared to these disciples on the first day of the week (Lk. 24:13), and this was "the third day since these things were done", would this not indicate that Jesus died on Friday? No! One day "since" Friday would have been Saturday; the second day "since" Friday would have been Sunday, and the THIRD day "since" Friday would have been Monday! Obviously this verse is no proof for a Friday crucifixion.

The disciples mentioned that it was the third day since "these things" were done. They talked about "ALL these things which had happened"(verse 14). They were talking about more than just one event. No doubt "these things" included the arrest, the crucifixion, the burial, and the setting of the seal and watch over the tomb. All of these things were not "done"—were not completed—until Thursday. Jesus, we have noticed, was crucified on the "preparation"(Wednesday). "The next day (Thursday), that follow-

that "was risen" is the past perfect tense— these things all indicate that the first day of the week is when Jesus appeared to Mary, not the time of his resurrection. This would have been more clear to every reader if the trans- lators had placed the comma after risen, instead of after week. Let us remember that it is the words of the Bible that were inspired by God, but the punctuation was later added by men and is subject to error.

ed the day of the preparation, the chief priests and Pharisees came together unto Pilate, Saying, Sir, we remember that that deceiver said, while he was yet alive, After three days I will rise again. Command therefore that the sepulchre be made sure until the third day, lest his disciples come by night, and steal him away, and say unto the people, He is risen from the dead: So that the last error shall be worse than the first." And for this reason, the tomb was sealed and guarded (Mt. 27:62-66). So then, "These things" were not fully completed—were not "done"—until the tomb was sealed and guarded. This happened, as we have already seen on Thursday of that week, the high day. Sunday was truly "the third day since these things were done", but not the third day since the crucifixion.

Since Christ was crucified on the day before the sabbath, we can understand why some have thought of Friday as the day of the crucifixion. But the sabbath that followed our Lord's crucifixion was not the weekly sabbath, it was an annual sabbath—"For that sabbath was an HIGH DAY" (John 19:14, 31). This sabbath could fall on any day of the week.

We believe the scriptures indicate that in the year Jesus was crucified that the high day sabbath came on Thursday. He was crucified and buried on the "preparation day" (Wednesday), the next day was the high day sabbath (Thursday), then Friday, followed by the weekly sabbath (Saturday). With this interpretation, we can understand how it is that Christ was crucified on the day BEFORE the sabbath, was already risen from the tomb when the day AFTER the sabbath came—yet still fulfilling his sign of three days and three nights! All of this becomes clear when we understand that there were TWO sabbaths that week—the annual high day sabbath and the weekly sabbath.

A careful comparison of Mark 16:1 with Luke 23:56 provides us with further evidence that there were two sabbaths that week —AND that there was a common work day between these two sabbaths. Let us notice first, Mark 16:1: "And when the sabbath was past, Mary Magdalene and Mary the mother of James, and Salome, bought sweet spices that they might come and anoint him" (A.R.V.[1]). This verse plainly states that it was AFTER the sabbath that these women bought their spices. The other verse, however, states that they prepared these spices and AFTER preparing them, rested on the sabbath. "And they returned, and prepared spices and ointments; and rested the sabbath day according to the commandment" (Luke 23:56).

[1]. The King James Version is the only translation (of many we have checked) that uses the indefinite "had bought". All others have correctly rendered this as "bought."

147

The one verse says that it was AFTER the sabbath that the women bought spices; the other verse says that they prepared the spices BEFORE the sabbath. Of course they couldn't prepare the spices until first they had purchased them! Sounds like a contradiction, doesn't it? But it's not! It all becomes clear when we remember that there were TWO different sabbaths that week! Jesus was buried just before sundown on Wednesday; Thursday was the high day Sabbath; and "after"this sabbath—on Friday—the women "bought" their spices and prepared them. After preparing the spices, they rested on the weekly sabbath. Then going to the tomb on the first day of the week, they found the tomb empty. Jesus was not there! He had already risen! Truly Jesus fulfilled his sign of three days and three nights. With this interpretation, the various terms used and the gospel accounts become complementary, not contradictory.

R. A. Torrey, a noted evangelist and Bible institute dean, years ago mentioned this truth about the three days and three nights. Since this was not the generally held position of his denominational brethren, he was speaking from conviction and not convenience. This makes his words in this connection especially significant.

In his book "Difficulties and Alleged Errors and Contradictions in the Bible" (written in 1907), Torrey said: "...According to the commonly accepted tradition of the church, Jesus was crucified on Friday...and was raised from the dead very early in the morning of the following Sunday. Many readers of the Bible are puzzled to know how the interval between late Friday afternoon and early Sunday morning can be figured out to be three days and three nights. It seems rather to be two nights, one day and a very small portion of another day.

"The solution of this apparent difficulty proposed by many commentators is that 'a day and a night' is simply another way of saying 'a day', and that the ancient Jews reckoned a fraction of a day as a whole day...There are many persons whom this solution does not altogether satisfy, and the writer is free to confess it does not satisfy him at all. It seems to me to be a makeshift...

"...the Bible nowhere says or implies that Jesus was crucified and died on Friday. It is said that Jesus was crucified on 'the day before the Sabbath'...Now the Bible does not leave us to speculate

148

in regard to which sabbath is meant in this instance... it was not the day before the weekly sabbath (that is, Friday), but it was the day before the Passover sabbath, which came this year on Thursday— that is to say, the day on which Jesus Christ was crucified was Wednesday. John makes this as clear as day...

"To sum it all up, Jesus died just about sunset on Wednesday. Seventy-two hours later... he arose from the grave. When the women visited the tomb just before dawn in the morning they found the grave already empty...

"There is absolutely nothing in favour of Friday crucifixion, but everything in the Scriptures is perfectly harmonized by Wednesday crucifixion. It is remarkable how many prophetical and typical passages of the Old Testament are fulfilled and how many seeming discrepancies in the Gospel narratives are straightened out when we once come to understand that Jesus died on Wednesday, and not on Friday" (pp. 104-109).

CHAPTER NINETEEN

Fish, Friday, and the Spring Festival

WE HAVE SEEN right from the scriptures that Friday was very definitely NOT the day of the week on which Christ was crucified. Yet each Friday many Catholics abstain from meat—substituting fish in its place—supposedly in remembrance of the Friday crucifixion. Roman Catholics in the United States are no longer required by their church to abstain from meat on Fridays (as formerly)—except during Lent—nevertheless many still follow the custom of fish on Friday.

Having seen how numerous doctrines and rites were adopted into the Roman Catholic church from paganism, we need not be surprised to find that numerous attempts were also made to "Christianize" certain popular pagan days and their accompanying customs. Has this been the case with Friday and fish? Certainly the scriptures never associate Friday with fish. On the other hand, there is evidence of the basic idea among the philosophies of the pagans!

The word "Friday" comes from the name of "Freya", who was regarded as the goddess of peace, joy, and FERTILITY by the ancient pagans.[1] And as the symbol of her fertility, the FISH was regarded as being sacred to her! Now the fish has from very early times been a symbol of fertility. It was a well known symbol of fertility among the ancient Babylonians, as well as the Assyrians, Phoenicians, the Chinese, and others.[2] The very word "fish" comes from the original word "dag" implying increase or fecundity.[3] The reason the fish was used as a symbol of fertility is seen by the simple fact that it has a very high reproduction rate. For example, a single cod fish annually spawns upwards of 9,000,000 eggs; the flounder, 1,000,000; the sturgeon, 700,000;

1. Fausset, p. 232, Art. "fish."
2. A Dictionary of Symbols.
3. Fausset, p. 232.

the perch, 400,000; the mackeral, 500,000; the herring, 10,000; etc. And so, from ancient times, the fish has been a symbol of sexual fertility, and thus was associated with the Goddess of fertility—Freya—Friday! Now we are beginning to see the real significance of Friday and fish.

The Romans called the Goddess of sexual fertility by the name Venus. And thus it is from the name of the Goddess Venus that our modern words "venereal" and "venereal disease" have come. Friday was regarded as her sacred day [1], because it was believed that the planet Venus ruled the first hour of Friday and thus it was called *dies Veneris.* And—to make the significance complete— the fish was also regarded as being sacred to her. [2] The accompanying illustration, as seen in "Ancient Pagan and Modern Christian Symbolism", shows the Goddess Venus with her symbol, the fish. The similarities between the two, would indicate that Venus and Freya were originally one and the same goddess— and that original being the mother-goddess of Babylon!

The same association of the Mother Goddess with the fish-fertility symbol is evidenced among the symbols of the Goddess in other forms also. The fish was regarded as sacred to Ashtoreth, the name under which the Israelites worshipped the pagan Goddess. [3] And in ancient Egypt, Isis is sometimes represented with a fish on her head, as seen in the accompanying illustration.

In view of these things concerning Friday being named after the Goddess of sexual fertility, Friday being the day that from olden times was regarded as her sacred day, and since the FISH was her sacred symbol—it seems like more than a mere coincidence that to this day, Catholics are taught that Friday is a special day, a day of abstinence from meat, a day to eat fish!

Now we have already noticed that Friday was not the day of the crucifixion of Christ and neither was Easter Sunday morning the time of his resurrection—as is so commonly assumed. Surely then,

1. Encyclopedia of Religions, Art., "Friday."
2. Ibid, Art., "Fish."
3. Ibid, p. 105.

this is not the true foundation for the observance of Easter. From where then does Easter observance come? Did the apostles ever observe Easter? Did the early Christians dye easter eggs or go to the bakery and buy hot cross buns? Did Peter or Paul ever conduct an Easter sunrise service? Where did all of these customs come from?

To begin with, let us consider the very word "Easter" itself. The word "Easter" appears once in the King James Version of the Bible: "... intending after Easter to bring him forth to the people ..."(Acts 12:4). The original word that is here translated "easter" is *"pascha"* which is—as ALL scholars know and recognize—the Greek word for PASSOVER and has no connection with the English word "Easter" whatsoever. (See ANY Bible dictionary.) The King James version is the only version of the Bible that has inserted the word Easter instead of Passover in this text. It is well known that the word "Easter" is not a Christian expression—not in its original meaning. The word itself, as the dictionaries and encyclopedias explain, comes from the name of a Pagan Goddess—the goddess of Spring. Easter is but a more modern form of Ishtar, Eostre, Ostera, or Astarte. Ishtar, another name for Semiramis of Babylon, was pronounced as we pronounce "Easter" today[1] And so the name of the Spring Festival, "Easter", is definitely paganistic, the name being taken from the name of the Goddess.

And not only is the name "Easter" of pagan origin, but we shall see that the traditional customs and observances of this season originated in paganism also. A good example of this can be seen in the well known usage of the Easter *egg*. From the "egg-rolling" on the White House lawn to the yard of the most humble home, eggs are colored, hid, hunted, and eaten—each year at the "Easter" season. But where did this custom of using eggs at this season begin? Are we to suppose that Christians of the New Testament dyed eggs? Do eggs have anything to do with Christ or his resurrection? The answer is obvious. Such usage is completely foreign to the Bible.

On the other hand, the egg was a sacred symbol among the Babylonians! They believed an old fable about an egg of wonderous size which was supposed to have fallen from heaven into the Euphrates River. From this marvelous egg—according

1. Hislop, p. 103.

152

to the ancient story—the Goddess Astarte (Easter), was hatched. And so the egg came to symbolize the Goddess Easter.[1] From Babylon—the MOTHER of false religion—humanity was scattered to the various parts of the earth and with them they took the idea of the Mystic Egg. Thus we find the egg as a sacred symbol among many nations:

The ancient Druids bore an egg as the sacred emblem of their idolatrous order.[2] The procession of Ceres in Rome was preceded by an egg.[3] In the Mysteries of Bacchus, an egg was consecrated as part of their ceremony. China, yet today, uses dyed or colored eggs in their sacred festival. In Japan, an ancient custom has been to make their sacred egg a hard brazen color. In Northern Europe in pagan times, eggs were  colored and used as symbols of the Goddess Easter. The above illustration shows two ways in which the pagans represented their sacred eggs. On the left is the sacred egg of Heliopolis; on the right, the Typhon's Egg. Among the Egyptians, the egg was associated with the sun—the "golden egg."[4] Their dyed eggs were used as sacred offerings at the Easter season.[5]

Says the ENCYCLOPEDIA BRITANNICA: "The egg as a symbol of fertility and of renewed life goes back to the ancient Egyptians and Persians, who had also the custom of colouring and eating eggs during their spring festival."[6] None can dispute the fact that the egg as a sacred symbol has been a part of pagan festivities from ancient times.

How then, we ask, did this custom come to be associated with Christianity? Its adoption into the Romish "church" is but further evidence of the great compromise that was made with paganism— a compromise to gain popularity with both sides! And as when other rites were adopted by the "church", apostate leaders attempted to find some similarity between the pagan rite and some Christian event; so in this case, it was suggested that as the chick comes out of the egg, so Christ came out of the tomb! Thus, fallen church leaders—void of God's Holy Spirit—told the people that the egg was a symbol of the resurrection of Christ! Pope Paul V even appointed a prayer in connection with the egg! "Bless, O Lord, we beseech thee, this thy creature of EGGS, that it may

1. Ibid,
2. Ibid, p. 108.
3. Encyclopedia of Religions, Vol. 2, p. 13.
4. Ibid, p. 12.
5. Egyptian Belief, p. 24.
6. P. 859, Art., "Easter."

become wholesome substenance unto thy servants, eating it in remembrance of our Lord Jesus Christ," etc.[1] And so another "mixture" passed into Babylon Modern and has in turn become a part of our present day customs.

Now even as the fish was associated with the Goddess as a sign of sexual fertility, so also, the egg was but another symbol of fertility. When we think about it, it is tragic that such vile symbolism came to be associated with Christianity, when in reality such things have no connection with TRUE Christianity at all! And even as fish and eggs were fertility symbols of the Mystery religion, so also is the Easter *Rabbit*— the Hare—a symbol of fertility: "Like the easter egg, the easter hare," says the Encyclopedia Britannica, "came to Christianity from antiquity. The hare is associated with the moon in the legends of ancient Egypt and other peoples... Through the fact that the Egyptian word for hare, UM, means also 'open' and 'period', the hare came to be associated with the idea of periodicity, both lunar and human, and with the beginning of new life in both the young man and young woman, and so a symbol of fertility and of the renewal of life. As such, the hare became linked with Easter...eggs."[2] Thus both the Easter Rabbit and Easter eggs were symbols of sexual significance, symbols of fertility!

Another custom that is closely connected with the Easter season is the baking and eating of "hot cross buns." Again, this appears—at first glance—to be a Christian custom because of the shape or marking on the buns of the *cross*. But, as we have seen earlier, the cross symbol is not a Christian symbol. On the other hand, as early as the days of Cecrops, founder of Athens, (1500 B.C.), such buns were used in the worship of the queen of heaven.[3] "The history of the cross bun goes back to...the LIBA offered to Astarte"—the Queen of Heaven.[4] In the days of Jeremiah, God rebuked his people for a practice in which "the children gather wood, and the fathers kindle the fire, and the women knead their dough, to make CAKES to the queen of heaven...Therefore thus saith the Lord God: Behold, mine anger and my fury shall be poured out upon this place"(Jer. 7:18-20; 44:17-19, 25). Now in these two chapters of Jeremiah, the word translated "cake" is *"kavvan"* meaning "bun." (In all other places in the Bible, except in these two chapters, the word cakes is translated from different words.)

1. Two Babylons, p. 110   3. Hislop, p. 108.
2. Article "Easter."   4. Curiosities of Popular Customs, p. 483.

154

And so here was some type of special cake—or BUN—as part of the Mother Goddess worship. These buns were very possibly made in the shape of a cross or marked with a cross, for this symbol was regarded as sacred to her.

Another Easter custom that is celebrated in many parts of the land is the Easter *Sunrise service.* The common assumption is that such services honour Christ because he rose on Easter Sunday morning just as the sun was coming up! But though this is widely believed, we have already seen that the resurrection of Christ did not occur at sunrise. It was yet DARK when Mary Magdalene came to the tomb on that first day of the week—and the tomb was already empty! (John 20:1). Since our Lord's resurrection did not take place at dawn, then surely this is no basis for sunrise services.

On the other hand, there was a type of sunrise service that was a part of old pagan customs connected with *sun-worship!* Now we do not mean to imply that Christian people today literally worship the sun in their Easter sunrise services. Nor do we say that the Catholic who bows before the monstrance sun-image and worships the round, sun-shapped host, is literally worshipping the sun. But what we are saying is that such practices are an obvious *mixture* of paganism with Christianity.

In the Old Testament of the Bible, God's people went into the Babylonian captivity because they mixed sun-worship rites into their worship. God showed this to the prophet Ezekiel. "And he brought me into the inner court of the LORD'S house," said the prophet, "and, behold, at the door of the temple of the LORD, between the porch and the altar, were about five and twenty men, with their backs toward the temple of the LORD, and their faces toward the EAST; and they worshipped the sun toward the EAST" (Ez. 8:16). Here then were people that had known God, yet they allowed this mixture of sunworship to enter in and defile them.

But was this worship conducted at SUNRISE? Yes. It was definitely a sunrise service, for the scriptures declare that they worshipped the sun toward the EAST. And of course the sun is in the east at early morning—at sunrise!

It was also to the east that the prophets of Baal looked in the days of Elijah! As we have already seen, the sun was regarded as the representative of Baal (the deified Nimrod). Therefore, when Elijah challenged the false prophets of Baal on Mount Carmel with the words: "The God that answers by FIRE, let him be God", he was meeting Baal worship on its own grounds—fire being regarded as the representation of the sun-god. And at what time of the

155

day was it that these false prophets of Baal started calling on him? It was as Baal—the SUN—made his first appearance over the eastern horizon; for it was at "morning", that is, DAWN[1] (1 Kings 18: 26). Of course no answer came from the sun-god Baal, so they continued until noon and the rest of the day.

Rites connected with the dawning sun—in one form or another—were known in many ancient nations. Those who made the Sphinx in Egypt, built it to watch for the rising sun in the east. From Mount Fuji-yama, Japan, prayers are made to the rising sun: "The pilgrims pray to their rising sun while climbing the mountain sides...sometimes one may see several hundreds of Shinto pilgrims in their white robes turning out from their shelters, and joining their chants to the rising sun."[2] And the pagan Mithrists of Rome—whom we have already mentioned—met together at dawn in honour of the sun-god.

Now turning again to the Eighth Chapter of Ezekiel in which the prophet saw 25 men looking to the east at sunrise, we notice that they didn't seem to think it mattered much if such an observance was mixed in with their worship. They evidently thought it was a "light thing." But concerning this, God spoke to Ezekiel: "Hast thou seen this, O Son of man? Is it a light thing...that they commit the abominations which they commit here?...and, lo, they put the branch to their nose"(Verse 17). This rite of putting the branch to the nose was also associated with the dawn of the sun in the east. This was an idolatrous ritual of holding up a branch of tamarisk (called barsom) to the nose at daybreak while they sang hymns to the rising sun.[3]

It is evident that such sunrise services were RELIGIOUS gatherings. But is there any indication that these services were conducted at the "Easter" season—in the *spring* of the year? Yes, there is! Actually, as we already briefly mentioned, the very name "Easter" comes from the name of the pagan goddess of SPRING—and this was the time of her festival. She was regarded as the goddess of the rising light in the east, as the very word "East-er" shows. "The english EASTER...is at all events connected with the east and sunrise..."[4] Thus the dawn of the sun in the "east", the name "easter", and the Spring season are all connected.

But to further see the connection between the sunrise services, the goddess Easter, and the Spring season, let us consider the following: In the old fables of the Mystery cults, their "saviour", Tammuz, was worshipped with various rites at the Spring season.

1. Strong's Concordance.
2. The Story of the World's Worship, p. 320.
3. Fausset, p. 304.
4. History of the Church (Schaff). Vol. 1, p. 373.

156

According to the legends, after he was slain, he went into the underworld. But through the weeping of his "MOTHER", Ishtar (Easter), he mystically was revived. And the sign of his supposed coming to life again, was represented in the springing forth of the vegetation—in Spring!

Each year a spring festival dramatically represented this supposed "resurrection" from the underworld: "The resurrection of Tammuz through Ishtar's grief was dramatically represented ANNUALLY in order to insure the success of the crops and the fertility of the people... Each year men and women had to grieve with Ishtar over the death of Tammuz and celebrate the god's return, in order to win anew her favor and her benefits!"[1] When the new vegetation began to come forth, those ancient people saw in this a symbol that their "saviour" had come from the underworld, and this coming forth was suppose to be the thing that ended winter and caused Spring to begin.[2]

Now turning once again to Ezekiel Eight, we find that along with the worship of the sun toward the east, the practice of weeping with Ishtar for Tammuz was also observed. As we read in verse 14: "Behold, there sat women weeping for Tammuz"! And then in the verses that follow, Ezekiel saw the sun-worship rites. So here, even the people that had known God, had mixed the Babylonian religion into their worship—weeping with Ishtar the "Mother" for the dead Tammuz. This was a part of the Spring Festival (the springing forth of new life, new vegetation, etc., supposedly representing the coming forth of Tammuz from the underworld.) And closely connected with these SPRING festivities were the rites in which men looked to the east—to the rising sun at dawn!

Now since the true saviour, our Lord Jesus Christ, *in reality* did rise (not merely in nature, plants, etc.); and since his resurrection was in the *spring* of the year—though slightly earlier than the pagan festival of olden times—it was not too hard for the church of the fourth century (now greatly departed from the true faith anyway) to merge the pagan spring festival into Christianity—attaching the various phases of it to Christ. In this way, it would appear to be a *Christian* Festival, yet at the same time, it would retain many of its ancient customs. In this way, both sides were coaxed into the professing "church." In speaking of this merger, the "Encyclopedia Britannica" says: "Christianity... incorporated in its celebration of the great Christian feast day many of the heathen rites and customs of the Spring festival"—the ancient pagan festival![3]

1. Man and His Gods, p. 86.
2. Festivals, Holy Days, and Saints' Days, p. 89.
3. Vol. 7, p. 859, art. "Easter."

The evidence then is clear: today's observance of Easter is not purely Christian. Its customs are plainly a MIXTURE—a mixture of paganism and Christianity. Some feel, however, that we can take these various customs and use them to honour Christ. After all, it is reasoned, do not most Christians think of Christ at this season? Though the pagans worshipped the sun toward the east, could not we have sunrise services to honour the resurrection of Christ, even though this is not the time of day that he rose? And even though the egg was used by pagans, can't we continue its use and pretend it symbolizes the large rock that was in front of the tomb? In other words, some feel we can take all of these pagan beliefs and ideas, and instead of applying them to the false gods as the heathen did, we will use them to glorify Christ. At first glance, this might SEEM like good reasoning. But this idea of adding pagan customs into the worship of the true God is utterly and absolutely condemned in the Bible! Here is what God says: "TAKE HEED... that thou inquire not after their gods (pagan gods), saying: How did these nations serve their gods? even so will I do likewise. Thou shalt NOT do so unto the LORD thy God... What thing soever I command you, observe to do it; thou shalt not ADD thereto..."(Deut. 12:30-32). Plainly then, our God does not want us to add anything to his worship. He does not want us to use customs and rites that the heathen used—even though we might *claim* to use them to honour HIM.

Having adopted the pagan spring festival of Ishtar or Easter into the fallen church, it was but a natural step to adopt the old "fast" that preceeded the Spring Festival also. Today, this period of forty days before Easter is known as *lent*. In olden times, these forty days were observed with weeping, fasting, and self-chastisement for Tammuz—to gain anew his favor—so he would come forth from the underworld, end winter, and cause spring to begin. According to the old legends, Tammuz was forty years old when he was killed by a wild boar. And so forty days—a day for each year he lived on earth—were set aside to "weep for Tammuz." The observance of this period of time in honour of Tammuz was not only known at Babylon, but it was also known among the Phoenicians, the Egyptians, and, for a time, even among God's old Testament people when they fell into apostasy (Ez. 8).

The forty days' abstinence of lent was known among the Devil-worshippers of Koordistan who inherited the spring observance from their early masters, the Babylonians.[1] Such an observance

1. Two Babylons, p. 104.

was also known among the pagan Mexicans who observed "a solemn fast of forty days in honour of the sun."[1] "Among the pagans," says Hislop, "this lent seems to have been an indispensable preliminary to the great annual festival in commemoration of the death and resurrection of Tammuz."[2]

Today, lent—the period of forty days before Easter—is likewise considered a very important part of Roman Catholic religion. But such a belief is not founded on the Bible, but is—as we have seen—a doctrine whose roots are in Babylonish paganism. As this paganism and Christianity were mixed together, little by little, the pagan "lent" was merged into the professing "church", only now supposedly to honour Christ instead of the pagan sun-gods to which it had formerly been used. It was during the sixth century that the Pope officially instituted the observance of Lent, calling it a "sacred fast", and ordered the people to abstain from meat and a few other foods for the length of its duration.

In our time, some Catholics may not eat chocolate bars, others may abstain from butter, another may smoke one cigarette a day instead of twenty, another may give up drinking during this time. But what *lasting* results are accomplished through such an observance? None. In fact, this is the very type of apostasy that Paul warned would enter in. He mentioned that when the departure from the true faith came, men would teach "doctrines of devils"—pagan doctrines—and especially mentioned one of these doctrines of "commanding to abstain from meats (foods)"(1 Tim. 4:1-4).

Of course, to the world that does not understand the "mystery" of all of this, they think that lent and days of "abstinence" are most surely of Christian origin and are of great virtue. But in reality, just the opposite is the teaching of the Bible and reason.

1. Humboldt's Mexican Researches, vol. 1, p. 404.
2. Two Babylons, p. 105.

CHAPTER TWENTY

The Winter Festival

CHRISTMAS—DECEMBER 25—is the day designated on our calendars as the day of Christ's birth. But is this really the day upon which Christ was born? Are today's customs at this season of the year of Christian origin? Or is Christmas another result of a mixture between paganism and Christianity?

A look at the word "Christmas" indicates that it is a *mixture*. Though it includes the name of Christ, it also mentions the "mass." Now the mass—with its rituals, elaborate ceremony, pagan prayers for the dead, transubstantiation rites, etc.—is most assuredly a continuation of paganism (as we have seen). Considering then that the name of these pagan rites, the Mass, is connected with the name of Christ in the word "Christ-mas", we imediately see an attempt to merge two conflicting systems together! Actually, to attach the name of Christ with the word "Mass", a pagan and heathenistic ritual, is but to pollute the Holy name of our God! And God says: "Pollute ye my holy name no more"! (Ezekiel 20:39).

The word "Christmas" is not found anywhere in the scriptures of course, and—as we shall see—December 25 is definitely not the date on which Christ was born. It is evident that our saviour was not born during the middle of winter, for at the time of his birth, the shepherds were living out in the fields with their flocks. As the scripture says: "There were in the same country shepherds abiding in the field, keeping watch over their flock by night"(Lk. 2:8). As is well known, the shepherds in Palestine do not "abide in the fields" during the winter season. The shepherds always bring their flocks in from the mountain slopes and fields not later than the fifteenth of October!

It is quite evident then that Christ was not actually born in the middle of the winter season. But, on the other hand, do the scriptures tell us what season of the year he was born? Yes, the scriptures indicate that he was born in the FALL of the year. For example, our Lord's public ministry lasted for three and a half years. (Dan. 9:27, etc.) His ministry came to an end at the time of the passover (John 18:39), which was in the spring of the year. And so three and a half years before this would mark the beginning of his ministry in the FALL of the year. Now when Jesus began his ministry, he was about thirty years of age (Luke 3:23). This was the recognized age for a priest before he could become an official minister under the Old Testament (Numbers 4:3). Therefore, since Christ began his ministry at the age of about 30—and since this was in the fall season of the year—then thirty years before this would mark his birth as being in the early FALL, not December 25.

While the scriptures do not tell the exact date of the birth of Jesus, there is a way to figure the approximate time of the birth of John the Baptist; and since John was born six months before Jesus, by comparing the two, we can again determine at least the season in which Christ was born:

John's father, Zacharias, was a priest in the temple at Jerusalem. During those times, each priest had a definite period of the year in which to serve in the temple. There were 24 such time divisions or "courses" when each priest would serve during the year. The names of these courses are given in 1 Chronicles 24:7 -19. According to Josephus[1], each of these courses lasted for one week, the first course began serving in the first month, Nisan, in the very early spring (1 Chron. 27:1, 2). Each priest in order would then serve his course. After six months, this order of courses would be repeated, so that each priest served a week— twice a year. Then three weeks out of the year, all of the priests served together—during the periods of the Passover, Pentecost, and the Feast of Tabernacles.

With these facts for our foundation, let us notice what *course* it was that Zacharias served: "There was in the days of Herod, the king of Judea, a certain priest named Zacharias, OF THE COURSE OF ABIA"—or in Hebrew, Abijah—"and it came to pass, that while he executed the priest's office before God in the order of his *course*...there appeared unto him an angel." The angel revealed that to he and his wife Elizabeth—though they were advanced in years—a son would be born. (Luke 1:5-13). But what time of the year was it that Zacharias served the course of Abijah? According to 1 Chronicles 24:10, the course of Abijah was the EIGHTH in order. This would have been Iyar 27 to Sivan 5; that is, June 1 to 8. Following his week of service in the temple, Zacharias was obligated to remain another week, for the following

1. Antiquities of the Jews, Vol. 7, p. 14, 7.

week was Pentecost. But as soon as this ministry was accomplished, he returned to his home in the hill country which was approximately 30 miles south of Jerusalem, and his wife conceived. (Luke 1:23-24). This was about the middle of June. By adding nine months then, we arrive at the approximate date of John's birth. According to this, John was born in the early spring of the year.

Now since Jesus was six months younger than John (verses 26, 36), we simply add these six months to the time of John's birth in the early spring and come to Mid-September as the approximate time of the birth of Christ. Again, the evidence indicates that our Lord was born in the FALL of the year, not December 25.

Still further proof of this conclusion may be seen from the fact that at the time Jesus was born, Joseph and Mary had gone to Bethlehem to be taxed (Luke 2:1-5). There are no records of this period whatsoever that would indicate that the middle of the winter was the time of taxing. On the other hand, there is evidence that taxes were paid in the fall season of the year. This was the logical time for the taxes to be paid since this was at the end of their harvest. There is also evidence that when Joseph and Mary made this trip, it was the time of a great feast at Jerusalem. This is the most logical reason why Mary went with Joseph—to attend the feast, as they also did on later occasions (See Luke 2:41)—for there was no law that required a woman's presence at a taxing.

We know that the time they went to pay taxes was also the time of one of the great feasts at Jerusalem because of the enormous crowd—so enormous in fact, "there was no room in the inn" at Bethlehem (Luke 2:7). Jerusalem was normally a city of only 120,000 inhabitants, but—according to Josephus—during the feasts, sometimes as many as two million Jews would gather there. With such vast throngs of people coming to the feast, not only would Jerusalem be filled, but the surrounding towns also, including Bethlehem, which was only five miles to the south. Mere taxation would not cause a crowd this big to be in Bethlehem, for each person returned to their own city to be taxed. And so, taking all of these things into consideration, it seems evident that Joseph and Mary made the journey, not only to pay their taxes, but also to attend a great feast at Jerusalem. This was at the end of the harvest season that they were taxed and this was also the time of the Feast of Tabernacles. All of this—as well as the evidence already given would mark the birth of Christ in the fall —not December 25!

Since Christ was not born on December 25, then how did this particular day come to be a part of the church calendar? History

162

has the answer. Instead of this day being the time of our Saviour's birth, it was the very day and season on which the pagans for centuries had celebrated the birth of the *Sun-god!* A study into this shows how far apostate church leaders went in their effort to merge Christianity and paganism into one apostate religion—even to placing the birth of Christ on a date to harmonize with the pagan birthday celebration of the sun-god! It was in the Fifth Century that the Roman Catholic Church commanded that the birth of Christ be observed forever on December 25th—the day of the old Roman feast of the birth of Sol—one of the names of the sun-god! [1]

In pagan days, this birth of the sun-god was especially popular among that branch of the "Mysteries" known as Mithraism. Concerning this we read: "The largest pagan religious cult which fostered the celebration of December 25 as a holiday through out the Roman and Greek worlds was the pagan sun worship—Mithraism ... This winter festival was called 'the Nativity'—the 'nativity of the SUN'." [2] And not only was Mithra, the sun-god of Mithraism, said to be born at this time of the year, but Osiris, Horus, Hercules, Bacchus, Adonis, Jupiter, Tammuz, and other sun-gods were also supposedly born at what is today called the "Christmas" season—the winter solstice! [3]

Says a noted writer: The "winter solstice (was) the time at which all the sun-gods from Osiris to Jupiter and Mithra had celebrated their (birthdays), the celebration being adorned with the pine tree of Adonis, the Holly of Saturn, and the mistletoe...tapers represented the kindling of the newborn sun-god's fire..." [4]

Now the fact that the various sun-gods that were worshipped in different countries were all believed to have been born at the same season (in the old fables), would seem to indicate that they were but different forms (under different names) of the original son of the sun-god, Tammuz, of Babylon, the land from which sun-worship originally spread.

In Babylon, the birthday of Tammuz was celebrated at the time of the winter solstice with great feasts, revelry, and drunkeness —the same way many celebrate it today! The ancient celebration spread and became so much an established custom that "in pagan Rome and Greece, in the days of the Teutonic barbarians, in the remote times of ancient Egyptian civilization, in the infancy of the race East and West and North and South, the period of the winter solstice was ever a period of rejoicing and festivity." [5]

When this mid-winter festival came to Rome, it was known as the Saturnalia—Saturn being but another name of Nimrod or

1. Encyclopedia Americana, Vol. 6, p. 623.   4. Man and His Gods, p. 201.
2. The Golden Bough, p. 471.   5. Curiosities of Popular Customs, p. 242.
3. Doane, p. 474; Hislop, p. 93.

163

Tammuz as "the hidden god." This feast was the most vile, immoral feast that ever disgraced pagan Rome. It was a season of license, drunkeness, and debauchery when all restraints of law were laid aside. And it was from this very feast at Rome that the merry-making of this season passed into the Roman Catholic Church and on down to our present civilization! "It is a matter of common knowledge", says one writer, "that much of our association with the Christimas season—the holidays, the giving of presents and the general feeling of geniality—is but the inheritance from the Roman winter festival of the Saturnalia...survivals of paganism." [1]

Tertullian mentions that the practice of exchanging gifts at this season was a part of the pagan Roman Saturnalia. When this mid-winter festival was adopted into the Roman church, this custom was also adopted. As usual, however, apostate leaders tried to find some point of similarity between the pagan and Christian religion—to make the merger seem less obvious. In this case, reference was made to the fact that the wise men when they came to see the Christ-child presented to him gifts. Some suppose that this is where the custom of exchanging gifts at Christmas time came. But not so. The wisemen did not exchange gifts among themselves. They presented their gifts to JESUS who was born king of the Jews. (It was an Eastern custom to present gifts when coming into the presence of a King.) But these gifts were not birthday gifts. When the wisemen arrived, it was some time *after* the day on which Jesus was born. By this time, he was no longer in a stable, but in a HOUSE. (Matt. 2:9-11). Obviously, the gifts of the wisemen were not *Christmas* gifts.

Space here will not allow us to enlarge on the use of the round wreath, kissing under the mistletoe, the use of the Yule log, the wassail bowl, holly, red berries, Santa Claus, the undue commercialism of the season, etc. , but all of these things are equally unscriptural and clearly identify our customs of today with the customs of the Saturnalia of pagan Rome.

And finally, in connection with the customs of the "Christmas" season, we will mention the Christmas *tree*. An old Babylonish fable went like this: Semiramis, the mother of Tammuz, claimed that overnight an evergreen tree sprang up from a dead tree stump. The dead stump supposedly symbolized her dead husband Nimrod; the new evergreen tree was the symbol that Nimrod had come to life again in the person of Tammuz!

This idea spread and developed so that the various nations all

1. The Legacy of Rome, p. 242.

have had their legends about sacred trees! Among the Druids, the oak was sacred; among the Egyptians, it was the palm; and in Rome, it was the fir, which was decorated with red berries during the Saturnalia![1] Among the Scandinavians, the fir tree was sacred to their god Odin. "The Scandinavian god Woden or Odin was believed to bestow special gifts at Yuletide to those who honoured him by approaching his sacred FIR TREE."[2] And even as other rites of the Yuletide season were absorbed into "Christianity", so also is the wide-spread use of the tree at this season a carry over of an ancient practice! "The Christmas tree... recapitulates the idea of tree worship... gilded nuts and balls symbolizing the sun... all of the festivities of the (pagan) winter solstice have been absorbed into Christmas day... the use of holly and mistletoe to the Druidic ceremonies; the Christmas tree to the honours paid to Odin's sacred fir..."[3]

In at least ten Biblical references, the "green" tree is associated with idolatry and false worship.[4] Now of course all trees are green at one time or another; apparently then, the references to the "green" tree refer to a tree that is especially noted for being green—the evergreen or a tree of that family!

Taking all of this into consideration, it is interesting to notice the reading of Jeremiah 10:1-5 and compare it with today's custom of decorating a tree at the Christmas season:

"The customs of the people are vain: for one cutteth a tree out of the forest, the work of the hands of the workman with the axe."

"They fasten it with nails and hammers.

AXE
HAMMER

"They deck it with silver and with gold."

Now of course the people in the days of Jeremiah, as the context goes on to show, were actually worshipping and idolizing the

1. Curiosities of Popular Customs, p. 242. 4. Dt. 12:2; 1 Kngs. 14:23; 2 Kings 16:4, 17:10;
2. Festivals, Holy Days, and Saints' Days, p. 222. 2 Chron. 3:6, 13; 17:2; Ez. 6:13.
3. Ibid, p. 238.

tree. We do not mean to infer that people who today place Christmas trees in their homes and churches are WORSHIPPING the tree. What we are saying is that today's use of the tree is plainly a carry over from paganism—in a much modified form of course. But whatever the difference may be between the ancient use of the tree as compared with present day customs, no one can deny that these things of which we have been speaking are customs of men. And God says: "The customs of the people are vain"—worthless, empty—they add no power to true worship.

Christmas was adopted into the Roman church during the fifth century. In the sixth century, missionaries were sent through the northern part of Europe to gather pagans into the Roman fold. They found that the 24th of June was a very popular day among these people. In order to induce them into the "church", as was the *usual* custom after the falling away, apostate church leaders would allow them to continue celebrating their pagan holiday, only they would attempt to associate it with some Christian event. But what event could they associate with June 24th? They had already adopted a day to commorate the birth of Christ—December 25th. And this error led to another error. They noticed that June 24th was approximately six months before December 25, and since John the Baptist was born six months before Jesus, why not set June 24 as the day to celebrate John's birthday? And this is what they did. To this day, June 24 is known on the papal calendar as St. John's Day or the Nativity of St. John! But obviously, such an idea is built on a false foundation, for John was not born on June 24; and mixing his name with this day was but a cover up, so the old pagan holiday could be continued—now within the "church."

In ancient times, this day was set aside for Baal worship. In Britain, before the entrance of Christianity there, the 24th of June was celebrated by the Druids with blazing FIRES in honour of Baal (the sun-god, Nimrod in deified form). The writings of such noted historians as Herodotus, Wilkinson, Layard, and others tell of these ceremonial fires in different countries. When June 24th was adopted into the "church" and renamed as St. John's day, so also were the sacred fires adopted and renamed as "St. John's Fires"! "I have seen the people running and leaping through the St. John's fires in Ireland...", says one writer of the past century, "proud of passing through unsinged...thinking themselves in a special manner blest by the ceremony."[1] In reading of such rites, we are reminded of similar practices into which the back-

1. Toland's Druids, p. 107.

166

slidden children of Israel fell when they would "pass through the fire to Molech"(Jer. 32:35; Ez. 20:31). Obviously, none of these practices had any connection with John the Baptist.

Besides the fire ceremony that was observed on June 24th, this day was also known among those heathen tribes as the festival of *water*.[1] And had not John the Baptist been especially known as the one that baptized with WATER? And so this slight similarity helped disguise the continuation of the pagan day, now renamed!

But the real significance that connected this day with water was that it was sacred to OANNES, the ancient Fish-god![2] Steming from another ancient Babylonian fable, as we mentioned earlier, Nimrod was supposed to have reappeared in the "Mysteries" after he was slain as OANNES.[3] In an article on Nimrod, Fausett says: "Oannes the fishgod, BABYLON'S CIVILIZER, rose out of the red sea," etc.[4] And so we see how Nimrod, water, and the fishgod Oannes were all connected. Now in the Latin language adopted by the Roman Catholic church, John was called JOANNES. Notice how similar JOANNES is to OANNES! And so by putting emphasis on certain points of similarity between paganism and Christianity, another pagan day was smoothly and cunningly adopted into the papal calendar, disguised with the name of John the Baptist!

We have already noticed in an earlier chapter how the worship of the ancient Mother-Goddess was mixed into Christianity. The pagans had for centuries prayed to and worshipped the Great Mother of heathenism. In order to bring these pagans into the fallen church, the ancient worship and rites that had been used to worship the pagan Mother were continued—only they were told to use the name of Mary, the Mother of Jesus, instead of the old names of Diana, Isis, Astarte, Artemis, etc. And even as other ideas that had been associated with the pagan Mother Goddess were merged into the "church" in an attempt to make Christianity and paganism appear to be one and the same, so also, August 13, the day of the ancient festival of Isis or Artemis, was simply renamed as the day of the "Assumption of the Virgin Mary" and right on up to present times, this very day is still highly honoured.[5]

As one writer speaking of this feast day of the Assumption of the Virgin says: "It is celebrated on August 13th; but that was the date of the great festival of Diana... with whom Isis was identified, and one can see, thus, how Mary had gradually taken the place of the goddess."[6] It is evident that the fallen church cared little about truthfullness as to *when* events actually happened. They

1. The Great Apostacy, p. 28.
2. Hislop, p. 114.
3. Bunsen's Egypt, Vol. 1, p. 707.
4. Bible Encyclopedia and Dictionary p. 510.
5. The Story of Civilization, p. 746.
6. The Paganism in our Christianity, p. 132.

appointed celebrations on the very days that were popular among the pagans.

Another day, supposedly in honour of Mary is called the Purification of the Virgin Mary or "Candlemas day", which is celebrated on February 2. On this day, Catholic priests pronounce blessings on *candles* which are then distributed to the people at mass. And on this day all of the candles to be used during the year in the Catholic rituals are blessed.

But how did the special observance of February come to be set aside as Candlemas day or the day of the Purification of the Virgin? This, like other days we have mentioned, was instituted in the "church" to replace a pagan day. And not only did the fallen church adopt this *day, but also its customs!* You see, in the early days of R o m e, this festival was observed by the carrying of torches and candles in honour of Februa, from whose name our month February is named! The Greeks held the feast in honour of the Goddess Ceres, the Mother of Proserpina, who on this very day was said to have sought her daughter in the lower world with torches! Among the Egyptians, this day was also observed in honour of the goddess Neith on the very same day that is known today as "Candlemas Day" in the Roman Catholic church! So the observance of Candlemas at this time of the year, its association with the Mother Goddess, and the use of candles are all beliefs that were *unmistakably* adopted from paganism.

These days and times we have mentioned—as well as numerous others which space will not permit us to explain here—were all adopted into the calendar of the Romish church from paganism. We wonder if the apostle Paul were to be raised up to preach to this generation, if he would not say to the professing church today, as he did the Galatians long ago: "Ye observe days, and months, and times, and years, I am afraid of you, lest I have bestowed upon you labor in vain"(Gal. 4:9-11). To what days did Paul have reference? The context shows that the Galatians had been converted from the pagan worship of the "gods"(Verse 8), and so it is evident that when some of them *went back* to their former worship(verse 9), the days and times they were observing were those days and times that were set aside to honour these *pagan gods!* And yet, it was these very days that the fallen church merged into her worship—changing them slightly, disguising them with Christian sounding names—and their observance has continued to this day!

1. Festivals, Holy Days, and Saints' Days, p. 27, 28.
2. Bonwick's Egyptian Belief, p. 115.

168

CHAPTER TWENTY-ONE

The Mystery of the Mixture

WE HAVE SEEN—by scores of examples—how it was a MIXTURE of paganism and Christianity that produced the Roman Catholic church. In the last two chapters, we have seen how many of our common, well-known holidays and customs originated. We have mentioned these things because they are so well known to us all that they are outstanding examples of how pagan customs were renamed and slightly changed to make them *appear* to be of Christian origin. And even as this was done with holidays and their observances, so in things *much more serious*—in DOCTRINE and WORSHIP—such mixtures were also made:

Even as the pagans worshipped and prayed to a MOTHER goddess, so the fallen church adopted this pagan Mother-worship also, attaching the Christian name of Mary to disguise the MIXTURE. The pagans had gods and goddesses associated with various days, occupations, and events in life. The fallen church adopted this system; but to make the MIXTURE less obvious, these "gods" were no longer referred to as "gods", but were now called "saints"—while the old worship continued! Even as the pagans used idols or statues of their pagan deities in their worship, so the fallen church did also, simply calling them by different names. From ancient times, pagans had used the "T" cross image, the initial letter of Tammuz, as a protector and an amulet. This symbol spread to the nations and took on various forms. The fallen church MIXED these superstitious uses of crosses with the cross of Christ. They continued to honour the cross *image*, while the true "finished", once-for-all work of the cross became hidden beneath the rituals of the pagan Mass with its rites of transubstantiation, sun-images, mystery drama, and prayers for the dead!

Even as the heathen had their repetitious prayers and rosaries, so these things were also MIXED into the fallen church, given a surface appearance of Christianity, and have continued to this day. The pagan nations had their relics that were highly venerated and which were believed to possess supernatural powers. The use of relics was also cleverly MIXED into the worship of the fallen church.

Pagan religion had its supreme Pontiff, so when paganism was MIXED with Christianity at Rome, this office—as unscriptural as it was—found a place in the fallen Romish church. The pagans carried their pontiff in procession; this practice was also MIXED into the fallen church. The pontiffs of paganism claimed "infallibility", and finally this too came to be associated with the Popes, the Roman pontiffs—in spite of the abundant evidence to the contrary! Even as the pagan pontiffs ruled over a college of Cardinals, priests of the Hinge, so does the pontiff of the fallen church. In literally hundreds of ways, pagan rites were merged with Christianity at Rome and this MIXTURE produced what is known as the Roman Catholic Church (as we have seen).

In his book "The Developement of the Christian Religion", a noted Catholic writer, Cardinal Newman, admits that: "Temples, incense, oil lamps, votive offerings, holy water, holidays and seasons of devotion, processions, blessing of fields, sacerdotal vestments, the tonsure, and images... are all of PAGAN origin"![1] However, because these pagan customs have been "Christianized"; that is, MIXED with similar Christian rites, days, or doctrines —renamed and rededicated—many reason that these things now receive God's approval. Catholics believe that even though a rite or custom was originally paganistic, that if it is applied to Christ, then it is acceptable to God, even though it has no scriptural basis! But this is mere human reasoning—a reasoning that is completely contrary to the written word of God! Let us notice this carefully:

Let us notice how this was the case in the days when the Israelites set up the golden calf (Ex. 32). None who read this account would deny that such worship as they engaged in was false, was heathenistic, and an abomination in the sight of God. They wanted a god they could see—a sort of supplement to their worship of the invisible and Eternal God. And so they set up the golden calf—a symbol of the son of the sun-god.  They sat down to eat and drink and rose up to play. They practiced heathenistic rites in which they made themselves naked (Verse 25). Whatever these rites may have been, they were no doubt rites that they had learned in the pagan land of Egypt, which in turn had received its paganism from Babylon. We have record that in

1 P. 359.

Babylon there were certain heathenistic rites that priests carried out naked.[1] Nevertheless, it is evident that the worship of the golden calf into which the Israelites fell was paganistic to the core! YET—and this is the main thing we wish to point out—they claimed that they were having a "feast to the LORD"—the true God! (Verse 5). Here then was a MIXTURE—an attempt to merge heathenistic rites into their worship and call it a feast to the LORD. Did God approve of this worship? We all know the answer. About three thousand fell by the sword as a result of such apostasy! Now if God did not accept such worship then, even though they said it was a feast to the LORD, then why should we suppose that he accepts worship today that is likewise a MIXTURE—a mixture between paganism and Christianity?

During the forty years of wandering in the wilderness, the children of Israel carried the tabernacle of God. They were strong believers in the true God, as we all know. However, some of them were not content with this, so they added something. They made unto themselves a Babylonian tabernacle that they carried with them also! As God said: "But ye have borne the tabernacle of your Moloch and Chiun, your images"(Amos 5:26). This apostasy is also mentioned in the New Testament where these idol gods they carried are called Remphan and Chiun, which are but different names of BAAL (Nimrod) and ASTARTE (the Mother-Goddess).[2] Because of this mixture, God rejected their songs of worship, sacrifices, and offerings. Though these were made to him—to the true God—yet such worship was not accepted because it was a MIXTURE.

To cite another Biblical example of how paganism and the worship of the LORD were mixed together, let us notice the Seventeenth Chapter of Second Kings. In this chapter, we read that the children of Israel fell into false worship. They instituted secret rites; built high places; worshipped the sun, moon, and stars; used divination and enchantments; caused their children to pass through the fire; etc. (Verses 9-17). As a result, they were driven from their own land. Then the king of Assyria brought men from various nations, including Babylon, to inhabit the land from which the children of Israel had been driven. These nations also practiced heathenistic rituals and God sent lions among them. Seeing that the LORD was against their paganism, they sent for a man of God that had been carried away in the captivity. They wanted him to teach them how to worship and fear the LORD. "Howbeit every nation made gods of their own" and these

1. In the Beginnings, p. 148; The Greatness that was Babylon, p. 182, 354.
2. Fausset

171

gods are listed in verses 29-31. They attempted to worship these gods and the LORD also—a MIXTURE. "SO"—in this way—"they feared the LORD, and made unto themselves of the lowest of them priests. . . they feared the LORD, and served their own gods"(Verse 32). Such worship was rejected by God—he hates a mixture. Even though these nations claimed to worship the LORD, they served idols also. Today, likewise, Romanism claims to worship the LORD, but it is obviously a system that is a mixture of idol worship.

In the days of Zephaniah, another attempt to merge heathen worship with the worship of the true God occurred. Concerning this, our Lord said: "I will cut off the remnant of Baal from this place . . . and them that worship the host of heaven upon the housetops; and them that worship and that swear by the LORD, and that swear by Malcham"(Zeph. 1:4, 5). Why was God going to destroy them? Were they not worshipping the LORD? Yes, but this worship of the LORD was mixed with Baal worship. God requires a pure worship and rejects a mixture-worship!

In the 17th and 18th chapters of Judges, we read that a certain man had a "house of gods"—a special chapel in which statues of pagan deities were placed. It had a priest called "father." The description plainly shows that such worship was idolatrous and false. Yet—and this we mention to show another example of MIXTURE—these people claimed to be seeking the favour of the LORD (17:3, 13). And the young father-priest claimed to speak the word of the LORD (18:6). So here again was a case of an attempt to MIX heathenism with the worship of the true God!

Another example of a MIXTURE of paganism into the worship of the LORD is found in Ezekiel Eight. Right in the very entrance of God's temple, the people had erected an idol. Inside the temple of God, even the ministers were offering incense to false gods. In this case, these abominations were pictures upon the walls— pictures of creeping things, beasts, idols, etc. This was plainly Babylonish, for such pictures are also found on the Ishtar Gate in Babylon. Also connected with the House of GOD were "women weeping for Tammuz"—the false Babylonian messiah—and men with their "backs toward the temple of the LORD, and their faces toward the east; and they worshipped the sun toward the east"—worshipping the symbol of the Babylonian sun-god! Now these people that had mixed such rites into their worship were people who had known the true God, the house of Judah (Verse 17). Though their worship was carried on in the House of God, though they prayed to God—the true God—yet God refused their worship (Verse 18). God does not bless a mixture!

In Ezekiel 23, we read of a time of apostasy when the people that had known God caused "their sons. . . to pass for them through the fire" and practiced other pagan rites. Concerning this, our Lord said: "Moreover this they have done unto me: they have defiled my sanctuary. . . For when they had slain their children to their idols, then they came the SAME DAY into my sanctuary to profane it"(Verses 38, 39).

Jeremiah also wrote of this apostasy. His message was to the people that claimed to be the people of God. These people when they came to the temple of the LORD, came "to worship the LORD" (Jer. 7:2). But notice that along with their worship of the LORD, other rites had been mixed in that were of paganistic origin! "Behold," God said, "Ye trust in lying words that cannot profit. Ye . . . burn incense unto Baal, and walk after other gods. . . and come and stand before me in this house, which is called by my name" (Verses 8-10). And this same people that came to the house of God, this people that claimed to worship the LORD, not only worshipped Baal, but the worship of the pagan Mother, the "Queen of Heaven" was mixed into their religion also! (Verse 18).

By repeated examples then, we can see from the scriptures that God will not accept a worship that is a MIXTURE. As Samuel preached to the children of Israel when they attempted to worship God and still at the same time hold on to paganism: "If ye do return unto the LORD with all your hearts, then put away the strange gods and Ashtaroth (the pagan Mother worship) from among you, and prepare your hearts unto the LORD, and serve him ONLY: and he will deliver you. . . " (1 Sam. 7:3). And this is still the unchanging message of our God today. Worship and serve the Lord ONLY, with no mixture of paganism, with no mixture of rites and doctrines whose roots are in heathenism!

Satan does not appear as a monster with horns, a long tail, and a pitchfork. No, to deceive people, he appears as an angel of light (2 Cor. 11:14). Likewise, when he wanted to continue his old paganism, he knew that to deceive the world, he would have to continue it in disguise! Thus, little by little, he caused men to MIX Babylonish paganism into Christianity. This was done very smoothly over a long period of time until paganism was established in what was called the "church"—now dressed up with outer garments that appeared to be "Christian." As Jesus warned about "wolves" in sheeps' clothing (Mt. 7:15), so pagan wolves took on

173

Christian garments—and this clever mixture has deceived millions. But even as we might remove the skull-and-cross-bones label from a bottle of poison and substitute a peppermint candy label in its place, such would never change the contents on the inside. The contents would be deadly just the same. So also is paganism deadly, no matter how much it may be dressed up on the outside!

Because of the clever way that paganism was mixed with Christianity, the true Babylonish origin of fallen "Christianity" became hidden—became a MYSTERY--"Mystery Babylon." But even as a detective gathers clues and facts to solve a mystery, so in this book we have presented many Biblical and historical clues as evidence to solve the mystery. Some of these clues may have seemed insignificant at first glance, but when the full picture is seen, these things all go together to conclusively solve the mystery of Babylon—ancient and modern!

We have seen that (1) Babylonian religion originated with Nimrod, his Queen-wife Semiramis, and her supposed god-child Tammuz; (2) as men were scattered from Babylon, they took this religion with them which developed in various forms and names; (3) when Rome conquered the world, these various phases of the Babylonian religion were absorbed into the Roman Empire becoming what is known in history as Pagan Rome; (4) then later, as history clearly reveals, much of this paganism was mixed with Christianity at Rome—a mixture which produced the Roman Catholic church; (5) the Reformation rejected a certain amount of the pagan element in Romanism, but still retained parts of it. And so today, much of what is called "Christianity" is still in a "fallen" condition—as the result of that great falling away of the third and fourth centuries that has deceived the world! And concerning this fallen system that is called "Mystery Babylon", God has spoken: "Come out of her, my people, that ye be not partakers of her sins..."(Rev. 18:4).

To whom then shall we look for salvation? Let us look to JESUS, the author and finisher of our faith, the Apostle and High Priest of our profession, the Lamb of God, the Captain of our Salvation, the Bread from heaven, the Water of Life, the Good Shepherd, the Prince of Peace, the King of kings and Lord of lords! "Neither is there salvation in any other: for there is none other name under heaven given among men, whereby we must be saved"(Acts 4:12). Our salvation then is not dependent on a human priest. It is not dependent on "Mary", the "saints", or the Pope! Jesus said, "I am the way, the truth, and the life: no man cometh unto the Father, but by me"(John 14:6).

Salvation then comes through Christ—and only through Him! Will we accept Him and obey His word the BIBLE or will we follow a religion that is built on "mixtures" that originated in BABYLON? Which will we choose?

BIBLIOGRAPHY

ABINGDON BIBLE COMMENTARY, F. C. Eiselen (ed.) Abingdon Press, N.Y.

AN APPEAL TO THE CHRISTIAN WORLD, Alexander Denovan.

ANCIENT CITIES AND TEMPLES—BABYLON, Albert Champdor.

ANCIENT MONUMENTS OF ROME, Theodore Pignatorre.

ANCIENT PAGAN SYMBOLS, Elisabeth Goldsmith.

ANNALES ECCLESIASTICI, Cardinal Cesare Baronius.

ANNALI D' ITALIA·(Vol. 5), Louis A. Muratori (ed.)

ANNUAL OF UNIVERSIAL CHURCH HISTORY, John P. L. Zog.

ANTIQUITIES OF THE JEWS, Flavius Josephus.

ARCHITECTURE, NATURE, AND MAGIC, W. R. Lethaby.

BABYLON AND NINEVEH, A. H. Layard.

BABYLON—JUST WHAT IS IT? J. Q. Adams

BABYLON THE GREAT HAS FALLEN, Watchtower Bible and Tract Society (c).

BIBLE MYTHS, T. W. Doane.

BIBLE STANDARD (Vol. 45, no. 2,5), R. G. Jolly (ed.)

BRYANT'S ANCIENT MYTHOLOGY, Jacob Bryant.

CAMBRIDGE ANCIENT HISTORY—EGYPT AND BABYLONIA, THE, J. B. Bury.

CATHOLIC ENCYCLOPEDIA (1913 ed.).

CATHOLIC PICTURE DICTIONARY, A, Harold A. Pfeiffer.

CATHOLIC WORD LIST, A, Rudolph G. Bandas.

COMPANION GUIDE TO ROME, THE, Georgina Masson (Harper and Roe, N.Y.)

CONCISE CATHOLIC DICTIONARY, Robert C. Broderick.

CROSS IN TRADITION, HISTORY, AND ART, THE, William Wood Seymour.

CROSS—ITS HISTORY AND SYMBOLISM, THE, George Willard Bemson.

CURIOSITIES OF POPULAR CUSTOMS, William S. Walsh (Lippincott Co.)

CUSTOMS OF MANKIND, THE, Lillian Eichler (1937).

DECLINE OF THE MEDIEVAL CHURCH, THE, Alexander C. Flick.

DEVELOPEMENT OF THE CHRISTIAN RELIGION, THE, Cardinal Newman.

DICTIONARY OF SYMBOLS, A, J. E. Cirlot

EARLIER AGES, James Harvey Robinson.

ECUMENICALISM AND ROMANISM, Peter J. Doeswyck.

EGYPT, Kenrick.

EGYPTIAN BELIEF AND MODERN THOUGHT, James Bonwick.

ENCYCLOPEDIA AMERICANA.

ENCYCLOPEDIA BRITANNICA.

ENCYCLOPEDIA OF RELIGIONS, J. G. Forlong.

EVERYDAY LIFE IN BABYLON AND ASSYRIA, George Contenau.

·FAUSSET'S BIBLE ENCYCLOPEDIA, A. R. Fausset (Zondervan).

FESTIVALS, HOLY DAYS, AND SAINTS' DAYS, Ethel L. Urlin.

FOX'S BOOK OF MARTYRS, John Fox.

GOLDEN BOUGH, THE, James George Frazer.

GREAT APOSTASY, THE, L. T. Nichols.

GREATNESS THAT WAS BABYLON, THE, H. W. F. Saggs.

GROWTH OF THE CHRISTIAN CHURCH, THE, Robert Hastings Nichols.

HALLEY'S BIBLE HANDBOOK, Henry H. Halley (24th Edition, Copyright, 1965 by Halley's Bible Handbook, Inc., and used by permission of Zondervan Publishing House.)

HASTING'S ENCYCLOPEDIA OF RELIGION AND ETHICS, James Hastings.

HARPER'S BIBLE DICTIONARY, Madeleine S. Miller.

HARPER'S DICTIONARY OF CLASSICAL LITERATURE AND ANTIQUITIES, Harry Thursdon Peck.

HEATHEN RELIGION, THE, J. B. Gross.

HISTORIANS' HISTORY OF THE WORLD, THE, Henry Smith Williams.

HISTORICAL TALES—GERMAN, Charles Morris.

HISTORY OF ARCHITECTURE IN ITALY, Charles A. Cummings (1901)

HISTORY OF THE CHURCH, Schaff.

HISTORY OF THE CHURCH COUNCILS, B. Hefele.

HISTORY OF THE CONQUEST OF MEXICO, William H. Prescott.

HISTORY OF THE POPES, Bower.

HISTORY OF THE REFORMATION, J.H. Merle D' Aubigne.

IN THE BEGINNINGS, H.R. Hays.

ISIS UNVEILED—A Master Key to the Mysteries, H.P. Blavatsky.

IS ROME THE TRUE CHURCH? S. E. Anderson.

JEWISH ENCYCLOPEDIA (1909 ed.)
JUDGEMENT OF THE GREAT WHORE, THE, Harvey H. Springer.
LADDER OF HISTORY, THE, Upton Close.
LEGACY OF ROME, THE, Cyril Bailey.
LIFE IN THE ROMAN WORLD, T. G. Tucker.
MAN AND HIS GODS, Homer W. Smith.
MEDIEVAL ITALY, H. B. Cotterill.
MEXICAN RESEARCHES, Humbolt.
MIND OF THE MIDDLE AGES, THE, Frederick B. Artz.
MONEY AND THE CHURCH, L. P. Powell.
MONUMENTAL CHRISTIANITY, J.P. Lundy.
MY DELIVERANCE FROM THE HERESIES OF ROME, Harry Hampel.
MYSTERIES OF MITHRA, THE, Franz Cumont.
NEW BALTIMORE CATECHISM, THE, Francis J. Connell.
NINETY-FIVE THESES, THE, (Harvard Classics), Martin Luther.
NINEVEH AND ITS REMAINS, Austen Henry Layard.
OFFICIAL REVISED BALTIMORE CATECHISM (No. 2), Ellamay Horan.
OTHER SIDE OF ROME, THE, John P. Wilder.
OUTLINE OF HISTORY, H. G. Wells.
PAGANISM IN OUR CHRISTIANITY, THE, Arthur Weigall.
PATROLOGINE LATINAE, Jacques Paul Migne.
POPES—A CONCISE BIOGRAPHICAL HISTORY, THE, Eric John.
POPES—THE HISTORY OF HOW THEY ARE CHOSEN, ELECTED, AND CROWNED, THE, Zsolt Aradi
PRIEST, THE WOMAN, AND THE CONFESSIONAL, THE, Charles Chiniquy.
REVELATION, H. A. Ironsides.
REVELATION (PRI), Robert D. Brinsmead.
RISE AND FALL OF THE ROMAN CATHOLIC CHURCH, F. Paul Peterson.
ROMAN CATHOLICISM, Loraine Boettner.
ROMANISM AND THE GOSPEL, C. Anderson Scott.
SACRED SHRINE, Yrjo Hirn.
SACRORUM CONCILIORUM, John Mansi.
SATAN'S GREAT DECEPTION, C. Paul Meredith.
SCOFIELD REFERENCE BIBLE, Scofield.
SECRET DOCTRINE, THE, H. P. Blavatsky.
SECRETS OF ROMANISM. Joseph Zacchello
STORY OF CIVILIZATION, THE, Caesar and Christ (Vol. 3), The Age of Faith (Vol. 4), The Renaissance (Vol. 5), The Reformation (Vol. 6), Will Durant. (Simon and Schuster, Inc., New York.)
STORY OF THE WORLD'S WORSHIP, F. S. Dobbins.
STRANGE SECTS AND CURIOUS CULTS, Marcus Bach.
THIS BELIEVING WORLD, Lewis Brown.
THIS IS THE CATHOLIC CHURCH, Joseph E. Ritter.
TRAVELLER IN ROME, A, H.V. Morton.
TWO BABYLONS, THE, Alexander Hislop, (Loizeaux Brothers, N. Y.)
VATICAN; YESTERDAY, TODAY, TOMORROW, THE, George Selders.
WINE OF ROMAN BABYLON, THE, Mary E. Walsh.